THE REIGNING ONES

Living as Heaven's Ambassador on Earth

Angeline L. Williams

Presented to:

_____

From:

_____

The Reigning Ones

Living as Heaven's Ambassador on Earth

Published by Redemption Books
www.redemptbooks.com

ISBN: 978-1-7325258-7-0
Published by Redemption Books
www.redemptbooks.com

Copyright © 2025 Angeline L. Williams
All rights reserved. No part of this book may be used or reproduced in any manner without written permission from the author except for the use of brief quotation in a book review or scholarly journal.

This title and other titles by author are available for quantity discounts for sales promotions, gifts, and evangelism. Visit our website or email us.

Book Design by Williams DocuPrep
www.williamsdocuprep.com

Scripture quotations marked NKJV are from The New King James Version. Copyright © 1982 by Thomas Nelson. Used by permission.
Scripture quotations marked NIV are taken from the Holy Bible, New International Version ®, NIV ® Copyright © 1973, 1978, 1984, 2011 by Biblica, Inc. Used with permission.
Scripture quotations marked NLT are taken from the *Holy Bible*, New Living Translation, Copyright © 1996, 2004, 2015 by Tyndale House Foundation. Used by permission.

Dedication

To the citizens of Heaven still discovering who they really are, may this book awaken the ambassador within you.

To every believer who has felt the tension of living between two worlds, longing for more, called to reign, and marked by Heaven, may you rise in the authority and identity Christ paid for.

And most of all, to my King, Jesus. May Your Kingdom come, and Your will be done, through every word and every reader.

Contents

Dedication 1
Contents 2
Introduction 4
What Is The Kingdom Of God? 8
   The Cross and The Kingdom 12
   Citizens of Heaven 14
   What Is An Ambassador? 16
   Prayer 19
   Declaration 20
Three Mindsets: Worldly, Church, or Kingdom? 21
   The Worldly Mindset 23
   The Church Mindset 24
   The Kingdom Mindset 25
   Mindset Comparison Table 27
   Reflection Questions: 28
   Prayer 29
   Declaration 30
Living From Your True Identity 31
   Common Lies And How To Renounce Them 37
   Prayer 39
   Declaration 40
Unlocking Kingdom Power and Authority 41
   Walking in Authority in Our Daily Lives 48
   Barriers to Walking in Authority 54

Reflection Questions 54
Declaration 55
Why Exercise Your Authority? 57
   How To Exercise Kingdom Authority In Your Daily Life 62
   Reflection Questions: 74
The Name of Jesus, the Word, and the Blood 75
   The Name Of Jesus 75
   The Power of the Blood 81
   Declaration 84
   Prayer 85
The Holy Spirit and the Kingdom of God 87
   Prayer 92
   Declaration 92
Living From God's Infinite Supply 93
   Faith and Action Produce Results 98
   Practical Steps to Live From God's Supply 103
   Stewardship 104
   Prayer 111
   Declaration 111
The Power of Kingdom Fellowship 113
   Practical Ways to Cultivate Kingdom Fellowship ... 115
   Prayer 118
   Declaration 118
Living with Dominion and Eternity in Mind 120
   Your Mission Is Where You Are 122
   Don't Wait. The Time Is Now 124
About The Author 127

Introduction

"For though we live in the world, we do not wage war as the world does. The weapons we fight with are not the weapons of the world..." —2 Corinthians 10:3–4 (NIV)

There's a quiet revolution rising among the people of God. It's not fueled by politics, power, or popularity, but by a deep internal awakening a revelation of the Kingdom. This book is born from that awakening.

For too long, many believers have settled for a faith that gets them into heaven but leaves them struggling on earth. We've shouted about salvation but whispered about transformation. We've prepared people for the afterlife while leaving them powerless in this life. But Jesus didn't just come to get us to heaven; He came to bring heaven to us.

When Jesus walked the earth, His message was clear: "Repent, for the Kingdom of Heaven is at hand" (Matthew 4:17). He didn't preach religion, self-help, or tradition. He preached the Kingdom. He healed the sick, cast out demons, fed multitudes, and raised the dead as demonstrations of a superior reality. Everything He did revealed what life under God's rule looks like.

Yet, somewhere along the way, many of us have never learned about the Kingdom or we've lost sight of the Kingdom. We've embraced church culture, but not Kingdom culture. We've pursued blessings, but not our identity as ambassadors. We've adopted the values of the world while claiming the name of Christ. The result? Confused believers, powerless lives, and a watching world that sees little difference.

This book is an invitation to rediscover what Jesus actually came to bring, the Kingdom of God and what it means to live with a Kingdom mindset. It's about learning to see, think, and live from Heaven's perspective. It's about walking in your God-given authority, stewarding His resources with purpose, and advancing His will on earth.

I know the struggle of living without revelation of who I am in Christ, of striving without identity, of enduring without success and how it can stunt your growth in this life in Christ. The Lord has shown me that when you truly grasp who you are in Christ and what you carry as a citizen of Heaven, everything changes. Chains break. Fear flees. Purpose ignites.

So let me ask you a sobering question. What reality do you usually live in? Do you live from earth, reacting to circumstances as they come, or do you live from Heaven, responding with the mind of Christ? Listen to these words from the apostle Paul::

> *"Therefore, if you have been raised up with Christ, keep seeking the things above, where Christ is, seated at the right hand of God. Set your mind on the things above, not on the things that are on earth." (Colossians 3:1–2 NASB)*

Paul's instruction to "set your mind on things above" means to intentionally anchor your thoughts in eternal realities. It means choosing Heaven's perspective even in the chaos of everyday life. But how do we actually do that? How do we maintain a job, raise children, pay bills, resolve conflicts, and manage life while looking into heaven?

It begins with "casting down arguments and every high thing that exalts itself against the knowledge of God, bringing every thought into captivity to the obedience of Christ" (2 Corinthians 10:5). We are to filter our thinking through His truth. We don't dwell on fear, gossip, comparison, offense, or shame because those thoughts were never meant to govern our minds. Jesus is our filter.

If we fail to set our minds on the things above, our thoughts become vulnerable, and eventually, our emotions follow. Before long, we will find ourselves filled with fear, frustration, anxiety, and every poisonous thing we've opened our minds to that's contrary to Christ. It's not just that we're thinking wrong thoughts; it's that our thought life is shaping our reality. Setting your mind on things above doesn't mean you won't face adversity; it means you'll be able to see over it.

This book is about much more than learning spiritual truths. It's about stepping into a completely new way of seeing and living. One that's anchored in Christ, empowered by the Spirit, and aligned with Heaven's agenda. You were not made to simply survive in this world. You were made to represent another. You are not just a Christian trying to make it. You are an ambassador of the King of Kings, sent to represent Heaven on Earth. The Kingdom is within you. Now, with Heaven's perspective and power, let's embark on this journey together, setting our minds on things above and waging effective spiritual warfare as ambassadors of the King of Kings.

Let's begin the journey...

What Is The Kingdom Of God?

"But seek first His kingdom and His righteousness, and all these things will be provided to you." — Matthew 6:33 (NASB).

The Kingdom of God is far more than a vague concept or a distant promise. It is a living, divine reality in which the rule, reign, and righteousness of Jesus Christ are actively at work both in heaven and on earth. From His very first public words, *"Repent, for the Kingdom of Heaven is at hand"* (Matthew 4:17), to His final commission, Jesus proclaimed a Kingdom that begins in the hearts of believers and will one day flood every corner of creation. That phrase "at hand" is not a call to religious rituals or external actions; it is a call to a change of heart and a new way of life in response to God's imminent reign.

When Jesus told Pilate, *"My Kingdom is not of this world"* (John 18:36), He did not mean that His Kingdom was irrelevant to our world, but that it originated from above, outside human systems, political power, and cultural trends. The Kingdom of God is spiritual, supernatural, and eternal, yet supremely practical and present now. The Kingdom begins in the hearts of those who believe and will one day be fully established across all creation

In parables Jesus described the Kingdom with seeds, pearls, treasure, and leaven because it is both hidden and powerful, internal, and external, eternal, and infinitely relevant to daily life. Wherever God's will is His Kingdom is manifest. The Kingdom is made visible through righteousness, peace, joy, healing, deliverance, and transformation. And the good news is it's already begun. But what does this multifaceted Kingdom look like in practice?

God is the sovereign King of heaven and earth, the Creator and Sustainer of all that exists. As Elohim, Yahweh, Adonai, and El Shaddai, He is omnipotent, omniscient, and omnipresent. These titles only hint at His infinite greatness. When Jesus taught us to pray, "Our Father in heaven," He was reminding us that heaven is God's domain: a spiritual realm more real and all-encompassing than the physical world it undergirds.

In that Kingdom, God's will is perfectly executed and His purposes are fully realized, both in heaven and on earth. When we yield our lives to His authority, we become active participants in bringing His desires to pass in our own hearts, in our communities, and across the entire globe.

The Kingdom is also God's jurisdiction: His ultimate authority and dominion over all creation, visible and invisible. Every corner of the universe belongs to the King, and every living being exists under His righteous rule. When we submit to His reign, we embrace our role as ambassadors who carry heaven's reality into every sphere of life.

The Kingdom is Heaven's influence. The Kingdom extends heaven's mercy, justice, humility, and love into earthly systems. As hearts are transformed, God's realities begin to permeate families, communities, workplaces, and cities.

The Kingdom is God's administration. Kingdom life is governed by God's wisdom and providence. He orchestrates events, resources, and relationships according to His divine plan, inviting us to steward His purposes under His perfect governance.

The Kingdom is God's impact and presence. The Kingdom is demonstrated by God's active presence among us. Wherever His love, justice, peace, and righteousness are experienced, the Kingdom has arrived, and His transformative power is at work.

So, as you can see, the Kingdom of God is not limited to one aspect of spiritual life; it encompasses a full transformation. It begins with repentance and being born again (Matthew 4:17; John 3:3), as entrance into the Kingdom requires a changed heart and spiritual rebirth. It involves the proclamation of the Gospel of the Kingdom (Matthew 9:35), spreading the message of God's rule and redemption to the world.

The Kingdom also brings healing and restoration (Matthew 4:23–24; Luke 9:2), demonstrating God's power to make whole what has been broken. Living in the Kingdom requires obedience to God's will (Matthew 7:21), not just hearing His Word but doing it. At its core, the Kingdom is marked by righteousness, peace, and joy in the Holy Spirit (Romans 14:17), reflecting the atmosphere of heaven brought to earth through the lives of God's people.

Jesus did not invite us to mere religious ritual; He called us to a change of heart, a new way of living in light of God's imminent reign. The Kingdom isn't coming someday. It's here now, and it will one day be fully established. As participants in this divine reality, we are called to be active agents living in submission to God's will, under His authority, influenced by heaven, governed by His wisdom, and empowered by His presence so that His Kingdom may expand in every realm where His name is lifted high.

In Luke 17:21 when Jesus said, *"The Kingdom of*

God is within you," He was preparing us to carry what He walked in. His life was a demonstration of how Heaven operates. Wherever He went, the sick were healed, the oppressed were set free, the broken were restored, and the outcasts were brought close. These weren't just miracles. They were glimpses of God's Kingdom in motion.

The Cross and The Kingdom

The Kingdom of God and the cross of Christ are inseparable. They are two sides of the same divine agenda. One cannot be fully grasped without the other. The Kingdom reveals God's eternal purpose: to dwell with His people, reign in righteousness, and restore all things under His authority. The cross, meanwhile, provides the path by which this purpose is fulfilled. It is not merely a historical event or a tragic moment of injustice; it is the central act of redemption in human history and the decisive victory in God's plan to reestablish His Kingdom on earth.

Through the cross, Jesus Christ did what no man could ever do. He conquered sin, defeated death, and reconciled fallen humanity back to God. He became the bridge between heaven and earth, the mediator between a holy God and sinful man. But His work did not stop at reconciliation. On the cross, Jesus disarmed principalities and powers (Colossians 2:15), stripping Satan of the authority he gained through Adam's fall. The dominion, intimacy with God, and righteousness that Adam lost in the garden, Jesus reclaimed through His death and resurrection.

The curse that was spoken over Adam and the entire created order in Genesis 3 was broken at Calvary. Jesus bore the weight of that curse so that we could walk in the blessing of Kingdom life. No longer are we bound by sin, death, or spiritual separation; the cross has ushered in a new reality, a Kingdom not of this world, but one that lives and grows within the hearts of those who believe (Luke 17:21).

The cross, then, is not merely a symbol of suffering; it is the altar of victory. It is the place where love triumphed over wrath, where mercy met justice, and where the eternal King secured His rule not by force, but through sacrifice. It is here that the promises of the Kingdom are fulfilled: forgiveness of sins, deliverance from bondage, healing of the broken, and victory over the enemy.

To proclaim the Kingdom is to proclaim the cross, for there is no entry into God's rule apart from it. Jesus said, "Whoever wants to be my disciple must deny themselves and take up their cross and follow me" (Matthew 16:24). The cross is both the entry point and the lifestyle of those who belong to the

Kingdom. It calls us to die to self so that Christ may live through us, advancing His Kingdom in power, grace, and truth.

The message of the Kingdom cannot be divorced from the message of the cross because the King Himself was crowned not with gold, but with thorns. His throne was a wooden beam, and His coronation came through suffering. Yet in that suffering, He reigned supreme, securing for us a place in His eternal dominion. The cross is the foundation of our faith, the gate into the Kingdom, and the source of our authority as ambassadors of Heaven. It is where Heaven touched earth and changed everything forever.

Citizens of Heaven

Paul says in Philippians 3:20 that *"Our citizenship is in heaven."* That is a positional reality for every Believer. You were transferred from the domain of darkness into the Kingdom of the Son (Colossians 1:13). You have a new identity, a new authority, and a new assignment. You are not a religious spectator, here to survive this world. You are a Kingdom citizen, a Kingdom representative, Heaven's ambassador sent here to bring Heaven to Earth. You weren't just saved to go to Heaven.

Living as a Kingdom citizen means aligning your

life with the King's values. Paul says in Philippians 3:20 that "Our citizenship is in heaven." That is a positional reality for every Believer. When you were born again, you didn't just receive forgiveness. Although salvation is great, being born again is not just about getting to Heaven. You were transferred from the domain of darkness into the Kingdom of the Son (Colossians 1:13). You have a new identity, a new authority, and a new assignment. You have access to divine authority, wisdom, and resources.

As you renew your mind to the Word of God, the world will see Christ: His heart, His character, and His power manifested on earth through you. They will see the beauty of living in the Kingdom of God.

So, you see, being born again is about much more than just getting to heaven. It is about bringing Heaven to earth through your daily life. It is about obeying His voice, pursuing His heart, and representing His character in everything you do, from how you raise your children to how you spend your money to how you treat the cashier at the grocery store. It is about allowing the light of Christ to shine through you beyond church services or spiritual settings. It is about allowing His light to shine in boardrooms, classrooms, living rooms, and neighborhoods. Anywhere the King's will is done, the Kingdom is present.

What Is An Ambassador?

Understanding the Kingdom is the beginning. The goal now is to move from revelation to activation. 2 Corinthians 5:20 says, *"We are therefore Christ's ambassadors, as though God were making his appeal through us."* You can't represent the King without exercising His delegated power. As Heaven's representative, you are called to reflect the rule and reign of Jesus on earth." Let's unpack what it truly means to be an ambassador of the Kingdom of God.

An ambassador is an official representative sent by a sovereign authority, typically a nation or a king, to represent their interests in a foreign land. In the natural, an ambassador doesn't speak for themselves. They speak on behalf of the one who sent them. Their words, actions, and even their presence carry the weight and backing of their home government. Now, apply that to the spiritual realm.

You are not just a Christian trying to survive living in the earth. You are a sent one, commissioned by the King of Kings to represent His Kingdom, His values, His power, and His love in a broken and fallen world.

Again, your citizenship is in Heaven. Philippians 3:20 declares, *"But our citizenship is in heaven. And we eagerly await a Savior from there, the Lord Jesus Christ."* You may live on earth, but your citizenship, authority, and assignment come from Heaven. As God's ambassador, you carry the atmosphere, message, and mission of the Kingdom with you wherever you go.

Here are some key traits and responsibilities of a Kingdom ambassador:

1. You represent the King's heart and will. You don't represent your own agenda. You reflect the nature of Jesus, His mercy, justice, grace, and truth. *"Your Kingdom come, Your will be done, on earth as it is in heaven."* (Matthew 6:10)

2. You speak with delegated authority. You don't speak your own opinions; you speak God's Word. You declare His promises, bind what He forbids, and loose what He allows. *"We are therefore Christ's ambassadors, as though God were making His appeal through us."* (2 Corinthians 5:20)

3. You carry heaven's culture into earth's systems. Ambassadors live in foreign lands but never adapt to the culture—they influence it. You carry Heaven's culture of righteousness,

peace, joy, and power into homes, schools, governments, and workplaces. *"Do not be conformed to this world, but be transformed..."* (Romans 12:2)

4. You operate and live under heaven's protection and with heaven's provision. Ambassadors are backed by their sending government. You are protected, resourced, and empowered by the Kingdom of Heaven. *"And my God will supply all your needs according to His riches in glory in Christ Jesus."* (Philippians 4:19)

5. Your life is set apart from the world, yet you are still engaged in the world for a divine purpose. Ambassadors engage the world without being entangled by it. *"Sanctify them by the truth; Your Word is truth. As You sent Me into the world, I have sent them into the world."* (John 17:17–18)

Being a Kingdom ambassador is not a metaphor. It is your Kingdom assignment. Every believer is called to this divine role. This world is not your home. You are Heaven's diplomat, sent to bring reconciliation, truth, and transformation. The question is, are you living like one?

God is not looking for fans of His Kingdom. He's

raising up *ambassadors* who will demonstrate it.

This book will equip you to do just that. But first, take a moment and reflect:

- Have you been living more as a consumer of the Gospel than a carrier of the Kingdom?

- Do you see yourself as an ambassador of Heaven or just a believer trying to make it through life?

- Are you reacting to life from an earthly mindset or responding from a Kingdom perspective?

As we journey through these pages, my prayer is that your eyes would be opened to the power, purpose, and presence of the Kingdom of God and that your mindset would begin to shift. Heaven isn't just your destination. It's your blueprint for how to live right now.

Prayer

Heavenly Father, thank You for inviting me into Your Kingdom. Open my eyes to see as You see. Renew my mind so I can think like Heaven, not the world. Let every area of my life come under Your rule and reign. I want to live not as a victim of circumstances, but as an ambassador of Your glory. Help me to walk in Kingdom authority, in Jesus' name. Amen.

Declaration

Declare these aloud in faith:

- I am a citizen of Heaven.
- The Kingdom of God is within me.
- I live from above, not beneath.
- I carry the presence of the King, And I release His Kingdom wherever I go.

Three Mindsets: Worldly, Church, or Kingdom?

"Do not be conformed to this world, but be transformed by the renewing of your mind..." —Romans 12:2 (ESV)

What you believe shapes how you live. Every decision, emotion, and response you have begins in the mind. That's why transformation always starts in your thought life. Before you can walk in Kingdom authority, you must adopt a Kingdom mindset.

Jesus gave us a clear priority: seek *first* the Kingdom of God. Not second. Not after we've chased comfort, influence, or approval. Not when it's convenient. We're called to seek God's Kingdom as our *first* pursuit—actively, diligently, and with intentionality.

This passage calls attention to two key words: "seek" and "first."

- **Seek**: Are you seeking the Kingdom? Is your

heart postured to chase after God's ways, not just His blessings? Jesus told us, when you diligently seek God in private, God will be diligent to reward you in public. God is a rewarder of those who *diligently seek Him* (Hebrews 11:6). What you pursue in private will be rewarded in public.

- **First**: We've got to be seeking His Kingdom and His righteousness first. Not after your job, or your comfort, or your plans, or even your Sunday service. Kingdom must come first, not somewhere in your top ten list, but at the top of it.

In the spiritual realm, there are three mindsets that shape how people live:

1. the mindset of Heaven,
2. the mindset of the world, and
3. the church mindset.

The mindset of Heaven is led by truth, driven by faith, and glorifies Christ. While the worldly mindset denies God and the Kingdom mindset advances God's will, the church mindset risks settling for spiritual maintenance instead of spiritual movement.

To live Kingdom life and as Heaven's ambassador, a Kingdom mindset is necessary. You must confront the two mindsets that can easily derail us: the church mindset and the worldly mindset. Both limit believers from walking in their full identity and calling. Let's break them down and contrast them with the Kingdom mindset.

The Worldly Mindset

The world teaches us to be self-focused, success-driven, and situationally ethical, where the rightness or wrongness of an action is determined by the unique circumstances of the situation rather than by what God says.

The mindset of the world is rooted in deception, driven by fear, and centered on self. It is shaped by the philosophies of this age. It is rooted in humanism, materialism, and independence from God. It says, *"Do what feels good," "Live your truth,"* and "Just be you. *You are enough."* It glorifies self, rejects absolute truth, and is driven by fear, pride, or desire. This mindset leads people to chase success, fame, and validation apart from God.

The worldly mindset prioritizes success over surrender, image over identity, comfort over calling, and popular opinion over God's Word. The Kingdom mindset, on the other hand, sees through Heaven's lens. It is built on faith, obedience, righteousness, and eternal perspective. It understands that God is sovereign even in suffering, that we live *from* victory, not *for* it, and that our purpose isn't just to survive, but to reign, serve, and advance the Kingdom of God on earth.

Paul warned about this in Romans 12:2: *"Do not be conformed to this world, but be transformed by the renewing of your mind..."* Attempting to live for God by applying worldly reasoning will only lead to ongoing frustration. To break free from the worldly mindset, we must surrender to God's truth and allow our minds to be renewed daily.

The Church Mindset

Then there is the church mindset. A church mindset acknowledges God, but limits Him to a building, a Sunday schedule, or a professional minister. While it values faith and community, it can become institutionalized and passive as Believers are confined to religious routines and man-made systems instead of being released into supernatural Kingdom purpose. They attend services as their spiritual duty and define success by church growth rather than Kingdom impact. This mindset says, *"I go to church"* instead of *"I am the Church."*

This mindset also breeds spiritual codependency. The people rely on the pastor to be their spiritual source. They don't really cultivate an intimate relationship with the Father. and the pastor may rely on the congregation for validation. Spiritual codependency is an unhealthy cycle that breeds spiritual stagnation.

Have you ever heard somebody say, or have you said, "I don't go to that church anymore because I just don't get fed there anymore." Well, guess what? The truth is that babies need to be fed. But mature sons and daughters of God rise up and take their place. They don't just sit in pews. They heal the sick, cast out demons, preach the Gospel, prophesy, and serve the broken.

The goal of the Kingdom is not bigger sanctuaries, but bolder saints. Kingdom-minded believers understand that the Church is not a building, but a "body" that is meant to move, grow, heal, build, serve, and advance. Jesus did not die to make converts who sit in pews. He came to raise up disciples who carry His presence and extend His rule. Wherever you go, *you carry the Kingdom.* At work. At home. In the streets. In schools. In hospitals. In prisons. At the grocery store. You are not a helpless citizen waiting to be rescued, but royal ambassadors sent to Earth *on assignment* with Heaven's backing.

The Kingdom Mindset

As God's ambassadors, we live in the Kingdom, under the authority of the King. We carry and demonstrate the Kingdom of God, which calls us to a higher standard than the worldly mindset, or even the church mindset. We are called to a standard rooted in divine truth, eternal perspective, and Christ-centered living. We are to view life through God's eyes and filter decisions, relationships, and priorities through His Word and Spirit. We are to reflect His values, will, and nature in every aspect of life.

A Kingdom mindset is so rooted in Christ that every decision, every response, and every motive is shaped with His presence in mind. It's asking, *"What does Jesus think about this?"* more than *"How do I feel about this?"* It's choosing to think, speak, and act from Heaven's reality rather than earth's reaction.

A Kingdom mindset is essential for living a victorious Christian life. To walk in the fullness of Kingdom life, you must first adopt Kingdom thinking. Romans 12:2 urges us, *"Do not be conformed to this world, but be transformed by the renewing of your mind..."* Kingdom thinking requires this daily renewal, where our minds are trained to think like Heaven and not like the world. This means aligning your thoughts, attitudes, and actions with Heaven's culture. It is not just about behavior modification; it's about heart transformation.

The Kingdom mindset does not reduce faith to

church attendance or traditions. Instead, it compels action, healing the sick, casting out demons, making disciples, and bringing justice. Believers with a Kingdom mindset see themselves as co-laborers with Christ. We engage in spiritual warfare and intercession from a place of victory rather than fighting towards it.

We know we are not just saved to go to Heaven, but we have been sent here to bring Heaven here. Our focus is on building God's Kingdom rather than seeking material gain. Jesus taught us to pray, *"Your Kingdom come, Your will be done on earth as it is in heaven"* (Matthew 6:10). That prayer is not just a poetic phrase. It is a mandate from our King..

The more we renew our minds to the truth of the Kingdom, the more we rise above the noise of culture and begin to think, speak, and live like Heaven.

Mindset Comparison Table

	Worldly Mindset	**Church Mindset**	**Kingdom Mindset**
Source	Led by culture and human reasoning	Led by tradition and routine	*Led by the Spirit and the Word*

Focus	Self-fulfillment, success, and personal gain	Going to church, receiving ministry	*God's glory and advancing His Kingdom*
Motivation	Fear, pride, or pleasure	Duty, habit, or spiritual consumption	*Faith, obedience, and purpose*
Ministry Outlook	Ministry is irrelevant or optional	The pastor does the ministry	*Every believer is a minister*
Power	Relies on self and worldly systems	Relies on programs or church structure	*Operates in supernatural authority and miracles*
Goal	Succeed in life on one's own terms	Maintain the church and attend services regularly	*Transform the world and bring Heaven to Earth*
Identity	Independent, self-made individual	Member of a church or spectator	*Ambassador of Christ and co-heir with Him*
Vision	Comfort, pleasure, and temporal success	Attendance, activities, and occasional service	*Discipleship, dominion, and eternal impact*

Reflection Questions:

So, with all that said ask yourself:

- Am I living to escape the world or to transform it?

- Do I see myself as a church member or a Kingdom ambassador?

- Am I living like a spiritual beggar or a Kingdom ambassador?

- Do I approach God with confidence or hesitation?

- Is my faith passive or purposeful?

- Does religion or a "church mindset" affect how I view myself in God's eye?

- Whose voice shapes my identity the most, God's Word, my past, people's opinions, or my own inner critic?

If things in your life seem out of order seek first His Kingdom and His righteousness and let everything else fall into place.

Prayer

Father, I repent for every thought and belief I've entertained that doesn't reflect Your Kingdom. Help me to see, think, and respond from Heaven's perspective. I surrender my mind to the authority of Christ. Reveal to me the lies and old labels of the enemy so that I may renounce them and replace them with Your truth. I want to fully embrace my identity in Christ. I choose to live from above only. In Jesus' name, Amen.

Declaration

Declare these aloud in faith:

- I have the mind of Christ.
- I reject the lies of the world and embrace the truth of God.
- I think Kingdom thoughts, speak Kingdom words, and live a Kingdom life.
- I am not conformed to this world—I am transformed by the renewing of my mind.

Living From Your True Identity

"But you are a chosen generation, a royal priesthood, a holy nation, His own special people, that you may proclaim the praises of Him who called you out of darkness into His marvelous light." —1 Peter 2:9 (NKJV)

Who are you, really? That's not just a philosophical question, it's a Kingdom one. Because how you see yourself determines how you live. And in the Kingdom of God, identity always precedes activity. You don't live righteously to become a child of God. You live righteously because you already are righteous.

Far too many believers are striving to become what God has already declared them to be. Instead of living from identity, they live for it, chasing titles, validation, or approval to feel secure. When you don't know who you are in Christ, you'll settle for every label the world, your past, or the enemy tries to assign to you. You must understand God isn't calling you to discover your identity through performance. He's calling you to receive it by revelation.

In the world, identity is earned. It's shaped by achievements, family background, job status, appearance, and social media influence. But in the Kingdom, identity is received, not achieved. It's established the moment you place your faith in Jesus.

The Word declares:

- You are a new creation (2 Cor. 5:17).
- You are God's workmanship (Eph. 2:10).
- You are a citizen of Heaven (Phil. 3:20).
- You are forgiven and redeemed (Col. 1:14).
- You are sealed with the Holy Spirit (Eph. 1:13).
- You are more than a conqueror (Rom. 8:37).
- You are a child of God (John 1:12).

These are not future promises, they are *present truths*. You don't have to work to become this person. You already are. The journey now is learning to live in agreement with what God says about you.

Satan is terrified of you discovering your identity

in Christ. Because once you know who you are, you'll stop settling for his lies. You'll stop giving your power away. You'll walk with boldness, clarity, and authority.

From the beginning, the enemy has attacked identity. In the Garden, his first tactic with Eve was to twist God's Word: *"Did God really say...?"* (Gen. 3:1). In Jesus' wilderness temptation, the enemy challenged, *"If You are the Son of God..."* (Matt. 4:3). The devil couldn't strip Jesus of His identity, but he did try to make Him question it.

He does the same with you. The enemy can't change the fact that you're chosen. But he' will try to convince you that you're unwanted and unworthy. He can't remove God's Spirit from you, but he'll try to make you feel distant. If he can get you to agree with a lie, you'll start living like it's true, even though it's not.

One of the greatest shifts that happens when you adopt a Kingdom mindset is moving from striving to sonship. In Christ, you are no longer an outsider trying to prove your worth. You're a beloved son or daughter with full access to your Father's presence and provision.

This truth changes everything:

- You don't pray for attention. You pray with confidence.
- You don't hustle for approval. You live from grace.
- You don't compete with others. You celebrate them.
- You don't walk in fear. You walk in boldness.

Romans 8:15 reminds us, *"You did not receive a spirit of slavery to fall back into fear, but you received the Spirit of adoption, by whom we cry out, 'Abba, Father!'"* Knowing your identity silences the voices of fear, rejection, and shame. It reorients your life around the truth that you are fully known and deeply loved by the King.

As indicated before, you weren't just saved from something, you were saved for something. God didn't redeem you just to survive life until Heaven. He redeemed you to reign with Him on Earth. It is important that you understand and accept this truth. Your Kingdom assignment is unique, but your foundation is the same as every believer's: you are God's child, His ambassador, and a vessel of His glory.

You represent the King not because you're perfect, but because you're His. What God says about you must have the final word, not culture, religion, or even your past. When you walk into a room, you're not just bringing your personality or skillset. You are bringing the authority, love, and presence of God with you. You're not there to impress people. You're there to impact them. That's what ambassadors do.

If you want to live with a Kingdom mindset, as the ambassador of Heaven you were created to be then you must allow Heaven to define you.

Consider this: if you call a lion a housecat and try to pet it like one, you're in for a rude awakening. Why? Because a lion will always act according to its nature, no matter what you call it. The same goes for an eagle. Identity determines behavior. And the same should go for you. Many believers still walk around declaring, "I'm just a sinner saved by grace." It may sound humble, but it falls far short of what God actually says about you. It may acknowledge your need for salvation, but it often keeps people stuck in defeat, shame, and passivity.

Yes, before Christ, you *were* a sinner. You were born into sin, shaped by a fallen world (Romans 5:19). But when you gave your life to Jesus, everything changed. The Bible declares: *"Therefore, if anyone is in Christ, he is a new creation. The old has passed away; behold, the new has come" (2 Corinthians 5:17 ESV).*

You are not just a forgiven sinner. You are a *saint*. Not perfect, but set apart for holy use. God does not look at you and say, "There goes that sinner saved by grace." No, He calls you beloved, righteous, chosen, and redeemed. You are His ambassador on the earth. And that new identity should shape how you think, live, and lead in the Kingdom of God.

When you keep seeing yourself as "just a sinner," you'll expect very little from the supernatural transformation that's taken place in you. You'll approach God timidly, hoping for crumbs instead of boldly receiving the promises He's already made available. But when you see yourself as a Saint, one who is set apart, filled with the Spirit, and called to purpose you will rise to that identity. You will live with boldness, pray with confidence, and walk with authority, not because of pride, but because you're living from the truth of who God says you are.

To fully live from your Kingdom identity, you must intentionally break agreement with the old lies and labels that once defined you. These lies often take root through painful experiences, repeated words from others, or our own inner critic. But when you were born again, you were given a new name, a new nature, and a new purpose.

Common Lies And How To Renounce Them

Below are some common lies people believe and how to renounce them and replace them with God's truth:

Old Labels & Lies	Kingdom Identity	Renounce and Replace
"I'm a failure."	"I am more than a conqueror through Christ." (Romans 8:37)	I renounce the lie that I am a failure. I declare I walk in victory through Christ.
"I'm not good enough."	"I am God's masterpiece." (Ephesians 2:10)	I renounce the lie of inadequacy. I declare I am fully equipped for God's purpose.
"I'm just a sinner saved by grace."	"I am a saint, made new in Christ." (2 Corinthians 5:17)	I renounce false humility. I declare I am a redeemed saint, set apart by grace.
"I'll never change."	"I am being transformed into His image." (2 Corinthians 3:18)	I renounce the belief that I'm stuck. I declare God's power is renewing me daily.
"I'm worthless."	"I am chosen, holy, and dearly loved." (Colossians 3:12)	I renounce the lie of worthlessness. I declare my value is defined by God's love.

"No one loves me."	"I am deeply loved by God." (Romans 5:8; 1 John 3:1)	I renounce the orphan spirit. I declare I am embraced by perfect love.
"I have no purpose."	"I am an ambassador of the Kingdom." (2 Corinthians 5:20)	I renounce purposelessness. I declare I am sent with divine purpose and authority.
"I'm broken beyond repair."	"I am healed and whole in Christ." (Isaiah 53:5)	I renounce the label of brokenness. I declare I am restored by the blood of Jesus.
"I'll always be anxious or afraid."	"I have a spirit of power, love, and a sound mind." (2 Timothy 1:7)	I renounce the spirit of fear. I declare I walk in peace, confidence, and clarity.
"My past defines me."	"I am forgiven and free." (Romans 8:1; John 8:36)	I renounce the shame of my past. I declare I am a new creation with a redeemed future.

Each time you recognize a lie, break agreement with it in Jesus' name, and speak the truth of God's Word over your life. This is how you renew your mind (Romans 12:2), and step into the full authority of your Kingdom identity. The more you meditate on and believe God's truth, the more you'll begin to believe it. And the more you believe it, the more you'll begin to live it. Remember this: God isn't waiting for a future version of you to use. He's ready to use the real you, right now.

Prayer

Heavenly Father, I come before You today with a heart open to Your truth. I repent for every time I agreed with the lies of the enemy instead of what You say about me. I renounce every label that didn't come from You—every word of rejection, every identity rooted in shame, fear, or failure. I cancel their power over my life in Jesus' name.

Thank You for calling me Your child, for adopting me into Your family, and for giving me a new identity in Christ. I receive Your truth: I am chosen, I am redeemed, I am set apart, and I am deeply loved. Help me to walk in this identity daily, empowered by Your Spirit and grounded in Your Word.

Let my life reflect Heaven's reality. I declare that from this moment forward, I will no longer live according to the world's labels or limitations. I will live from the identity You have given me as Your ambassador on the earth. In Jesus' name, Amen.

Declaration

Declare these aloud in faith:

- I am a child of God. Chosen, redeemed, equipped, and empowered by the Spirit to fulfill Heaven's assignment on earth.

- I am not defined by my past, my pain, or my performance. I reject every lie that contradicts God's truth.

- I walk boldly in my Kingdom identity, bringing light, hope, and transformation everywhere I go.

- I am a child of the King, and I live from that truth today and every day. In Jesus' name, Amen.

Unlocking Kingdom Power and Authority

Behold, I give you authority to trample on serpents and scorpions, and over all the power of the enemy, and nothing shall by any means hurt you." —Luke 10:19 (NKJV)

Kingdom Authority does not originate with us. All authority belongs to God. God gives authority when we are under His authority. This is not a power that we control, but an authority that we steward as we walk under the direction of the Holy Spirit in full submission to Him and His Word. Jesus made this clear when He said, *"All authority in heaven and on earth has been given to Me. Therefore go..."* (Matt. 28:18–19). That means the authority you walk in is delegated to you by Jesus. He gave you the right to act in His name.

Kingdom authority is not about our personal strength, titles, or earthly status. It flows from the King. As a born-again Believer, you have been filled and anointed with the Holy Spirit. This gives you Kingdom authority as a child of God, adopted through the blood of Jesus.

"...we are children of God, and if children, then heirs—heirs of God and joint heirs with Christ, if indeed we suffer with Him, that we may also be glorified together."—Romans 8:16-17

There is a significant distinction between power and authority. Power refers to the ability to influence or control outcomes, while authority is the right to use that power. Power alone can force actions, but authority carries weight because it is rooted in legitimacy, relationship, and submission to God. Authority is the ability to rule, and it is the basis of the Kingdom of God. Kings rule through authority, but they conquer through power.

As followers of Jesus, we have been given both power and authority through the Holy Spirit, not just to confront darkness, but to fulfill our Kingdom assignments with confidence and effectiveness. This means that authority is more than just a church concept or Bible lesson; it is a daily reality for every believer in Christ. In Hebrew, the word for authority means "having dominion, the ability or power to do something based on a higher power, or to multiply."

Power is the ability to see it accomplished.

The Greek word for authority is ἐξουσία (exousia), which translates to "authority" or "power" in English. In the New Testament, it refers to the right to govern, judge, and act in God-ordained freedom. Authority is spiritual dominion; it's the freedom to act within God's boundaries. It is the privilege and control that comes from God's delegation.

Many believers wonder why their prayers sometimes go unanswered, or why demons don't leave despite their commands. The answer lies in understanding the difference between power and authority. You cannot command demons solely with power, you need authority. The enemy is not afraid of mere noise or repetition; demons obey authority. They don't obey power. You command demons with authority. You don't do it with power.

In Luke 4:36, after Jesus came back from the wilderness, He began His ministry. The people were astonished by His authority and power:

> *"Then they were all amazed and spoke among themselves, saying, 'What a word this is! For with authority and power He commands the unclean spirits, and they come out.'"*

Later, in Luke 4:40-41, we see Jesus healing the sick and casting out demons:

> *"When the sun was setting, all those who had any that were sick with various diseases brought them to Him; and He laid His hands on every one of them and healed them. And demons also came out of many, crying out and saying, 'You are the Christ, the Son of God!' And He, rebuking them, did not allow them to speak, for they knew that He was the Christ."*

The people marveled because Jesus' carried both power and authority. His very being exuded the reality of the Kingdom of God. The demons shrieked as they recognized Him for who He was, even before He spoke.

When you understand both power and authority, you will recognize the difference in how you operate as a believer. Power is like a tool, but authority is the right to wield it. Jesus never intended for us to live the Christian life without help which is why He sent the Holy Spirit to empower us and equip us for Kingdom work.

When Jesus sent the disciples out in Luke 9:1, He gave them both power (dunamis) and authority (exousia) to drive out demons and heal the sick. This same power and authority has been passed down to us. The question is not whether we have it, but whether we understand it and walk in it.

This is the essence of Kingdom authority. Through the Holy Spirit, the power and authority of Christ dwell within you. As ambassadors of the Kingdom, we are called not just to wield power but to exercise authority, to enforce the will of Heaven on Earth.

Jesus never intended for His disciples to live powerless lives. He commissioned us to demonstrate the authority and power of His Kingdom as a living witness to a broken and dark world, but many believers don't. The problem isn't the absence of authority. Many believers either don't realize they have been given this authority, or they don't know how to unlock and exercise it. Through Christ, you've been entrusted with Kingdom authority to represent God's rule on the earth.

Again, understanding the source of authority is crucial in our walk as believers. Authority is not a mere possession; it is a responsibility that comes from being rightly aligned with the ultimate Source. One of the clearest illustrations of this can be found in the story of the Roman centurion in Matthew chapter 8, a powerful example that not only demonstrates Jesus's authority but also teaches us how authority is recognized and understood.

When the centurion approached Jesus, asking for healing for his paralyzed servant, he said something that astounded Jesus:

> *"Lord, I do not deserve to have you come under my roof. But just say the word, and my servant will be healed. For I myself am a man under authority, with soldiers under me. I tell this one, 'Go,' and he goes; and that one, 'Come,' and he comes..."* — Matthew 8:8-9 (NIV)

What was remarkable about the centurion's statement wasn't his understanding of healing, but rather his comprehension of authority. As a Roman officer, he understood that his authority over his soldiers came from being under the authority of Caesar. His orders carried weight not because of his personal power but because of the authority of the empire that he represented.

In the same way, he recognized that Jesus, who was under the authority of God, carried divine authority that transcended physical proximity and circumstances. Jesus didn't need to be physically present to heal; His authority was supreme and could act across any distance.

This encounter reveals an essential Kingdom principle: you can only walk in authority to the degree that you are under authority. The centurion's authority came because he was submitted to Caesar. Similarly, we, as Kingdom citizens, have authority because we are submitted to Christ. Our authority comes from our position under His Lordship. As we yield to His authority, we, in turn, are entrusted with the power to execute His will on earth.

Another profound example of Jesus's authority can be seen in the moment when He calmed the storm on the Sea of Galilee. In Mark 4:39, Jesus stood up in the midst of a violent storm and commanded, *"Peace, be still."* Immediately, the winds ceased, and the sea became calm.

The Greek word for "peace" here is εἰρήνη (eirēnē), pronounced ay-RAY-nay. It goes beyond the mere absence of conflict or war; it encompasses harmony, tranquility, and even a state of well-being and prosperity. Similarly, the Hebrew word shalom, often translated as "peace," carries an even deeper meaning. Shalom signifies wholeness, completeness, physical safety, inner tranquility, and harmonious relationships.

So, when Jesus spoke to the storm, His words were more than a simple command for quiet; He was declaring the removal of chaos and anarchy, inviting peace, wholeness, and divine order into the situation. The storm's fury was a manifestation of the chaos that this world often presents, but Jesus's command represented the Kingdom of God's authority, which supersedes every force of disorder and disturbance.

In both of these examples, whether it's the centurion recognizing Jesus's authority or Jesus calming the storm, we see the same truth: Jesus's authority is not of this world. It is divine, it is absolute, and it brings peace, order, and restoration. As followers of Christ, we too are called to walk in that same authority. We are called to be ambassadors of peace, carrying the Kingdom's authority into the chaos of the world and establishing the rule of God wherever we go.

Walking in Authority in Our Daily Lives

Kingdom authority is not just a theoretical concept. It is something we actively walk in and apply in our lives. Living under God's authority gives us the right and the power to bring His Kingdom to earth. Every area of life is touched by this authority: our thoughts, emotions, relationships, finances, health, and purpose.

This means that when we face storms in our lives, whether they are physical, emotional, or spiritual, we can speak with authority, just as Jesus did, and bring peace into those situations. It means we don't have to be ruled by the circumstances or the enemy's tactics. We have the authority to stand firm in Christ's victory. As we align ourselves with His will and submit to His authority, we also receive the power to fulfill His purposes on earth.

As we step out in faith, applying these Kingdom principles, we will begin to see transformation, not only in our lives but in the world around us. Remember: The Kingdom of God is within you, and you have the authority to bring Heaven's reality to earth. Take action today, and begin to walk in the power and authority Christ has entrusted to you!

Our authority is exercised in daily life through:

1. **Obedience**: Walking in obedience to God's Word and leading, submitting ourselves to His authority first and foremost.
2. **Faith**: Trusting that His authority is greater than any challenge we face.
3. **Action**: Speaking His truth, praying with

power, and living with Kingdom purpose.

When we walk in this authority, we carry with us the Kingdom's peace, bringing shalom wherever we go. This is the essence of what it means to live as Heaven's ambassadors on earth. Many believers today attempt to exercise authority over spiritual matters without fully yielding to the authority of Jesus. But submission to God is not optional, it's essential. Scripture makes this clear: *"Submit yourselves therefore to God. Resist the devil, and he will flee from you" (James 4:7 ESV).*

Notice that submission comes before resistance. The devil doesn't flee from self-willed believers. He flees from submitted believers, those who are under Kingdom authority and know how to wield it.

Authority in the Kingdom is not about shouting louder, quoting more Scripture, or displaying charisma. It's about knowing who you are under, and acting with the confidence that comes from that alignment.

To walk in Kingdom authority:

- You must recognize the source of your authority: Jesus Christ.
- You must stay submitted to His Lordship

daily.

- You must speak with confidence, not because of your strength, but because of His.

The centurion didn't need Jesus to perform a ritual or come to his house. He understood that a word from the King was enough. Do you believe that today? That the authority of Jesus is enough to heal, deliver, and restore by His Word?

Kingdom authority, the delegated power to act on God's behalf, only comes through a personal relationship with Jesus Christ. True authority is never detached from intimacy with the King. It is not a skill to be mastered or a formula to be repeated. It cannot be learned, manufactured, memorized, or mimicked. It is the overflow of a life fully surrendered in obedience and communion with King Jesus. The more intimately you walk with Jesus and yield to the Holy Spirit, the more confidently and effectively you'll walk in the authority He has entrusted to you. Intimacy is the foundation. Authority is the fruit.

Many long to operate in spiritual power to heal the sick, cast out demons, and release Heaven on earth, but they neglect the essential foundation: intimacy with the King. Kingdom authority is not about outward expressions; it's about inward transformation.

In Acts chapter 19, we see a powerful example of what happens when people try to exercise authority without relationship. The seven sons of Sceva attempted to cast out a demon *"in the name of Jesus whom Paul preaches,"* but they had no intimacy with the One whose name they were invoking. *"Jesus I know, and Paul I know about, but who are you?"* (Acts 19:15 NIV)

They used the right words, but there was no spiritual weight behind them. They lacked covenant. They lacked connection. And the result? They were overpowered and humiliated. This account is a sobering reminder. The enemy knows who carries real authority. He knows when you're just quoting verses and when you're standing in the reality of them.

Kingdom authority is not measured by how loudly you pray or how eloquently you speak, but by how deeply your heart is surrendered. Authority flows from abiding. Jesus made this clear in John 15: *"Abide in Me, and I in you... apart from Me you can do nothing"* (John 15:4–5 NASB). Abiding is a relational posture, not a religious routine. It's about moment-by-moment dependence on Christ, thinking His thoughts, doing His will, and remaining deeply connected to Him.

As we cultivate daily fellowship with Jesus and

live in step with the Holy Spirit, we are transformed into vessels of His Kingdom authority. Kingdom authority isn't about performance; it is about presence. It is the result of being with Him, becoming like Him, and being sent by Him.

Authority that's unlocked through intimacy is authority that carries weight. The more time you spend with someone, the more you begin to reflect them. The same is true with God. When you walk closely with Jesus, you begin to think like Him, speak like Him, and act from His heart. Your authority becomes a reflection of His presence in your life. This kind of authority isn't loud or showy, it's effective. It's not performative; it's transformative. Intimacy allows you to hear Heaven clearly and release Heaven boldly.

Obedience is the pathway to power. Jesus said, *"If you love Me, you will keep My commandments"* (John 14:15). Love is proven through obedience. Authority isn't given to those who simply know the Word. It is given to those who live it. When your heart is aligned with God's heart, and your will is submitted to His will, He entrusts you with the keys of the Kingdom. You don't need to shout louder. You just need to be closer.

Barriers to Walking in Authority

Sometimes, believers don't feel like they're walking in authority. Here are some common reasons why:

- **Ignorance**: You can't use what you don't know you have.

- **Unbelief**: If you don't believe you have authority, you won't walk in it.

- **Sin**: Willful disobedience can short-circuit your spiritual effectiveness.

- **Fear**: Fear causes you to shrink back when God is calling you to step forward.

- **Passivity**: Authority must be actively used, not just acknowledged.

Authority is like a key, it only works when you put it in the lock and turn it. To unlock authority, we must renew our minds with truth and align our lives with obedience.

Reflection Questions

1. How would you describe your current level of intimacy with Jesus and the Holy Spirit? What spiritual habits or distractions may be helping

or hindering your connection?

2. Have you ever tried to exercise spiritual authority without a deep connection to Christ? What was the result, and what did you learn?

3. In what areas of your life are you seeking more spiritual authority (e.g., family, ministry, healing, deliverance)? How can you grow in intimacy with the King in those areas?

4. What does "abiding in Christ" practically look like for you on a daily basis? Are there ways you can deepen that abiding relationship?

5. How does the story of the seven sons of Sceva challenge your perspective on spiritual authority? What changes might God be prompting you to make?

Declaration

Declare these aloud in faith:

- I am a child of the King, and I walk in the authority that flows from my relationship with Jesus.

- I don't need to strive or pretend. I abide. As I draw near to the Lord in intimacy and obedience, His power is released through me. The enemy recognizes the authority I carry because I am known in Heaven and feared in Hell.

- My words carry weight because they are rooted in covenant, not performance.

- I am not moved by fear, pride, or pretense.

- I abide in Christ, and from that place, I rule and reign with Him.

Why Exercise Your Authority?

"Behold, I give you authority to trample on serpents and scorpions, and over all the power of the enemy, and nothing shall by any means hurt you." — Luke 10:19 (NKJV)

When you decided to follow Jesus, you didn't just join a community you enlisted in a kingdom. And immediately, you became a threat to the kingdom of darkness. Whether you feel like a warrior or not, the moment you chose Christ, a spiritual target was placed on your back. You may wonder, *"Can't I just avoid confrontation? Can't I stay out of the fight?"* The answer is simple: No. There is no neutral ground in the spiritual realm. You're either advancing the Kingdom of God or being pushed back by the enemy. This is why every believer must rise and exercise their God-given authority.

Jesus didn't suggest that we walk in authority. He commanded it. In Luke 10:19, He said: *"Behold, I give you authority to trample on serpents and scorpions, and over all the power of the enemy..." "... go ... And as ye go, preach, saying, The kingdom of heaven is at hand. Heal the sick, cleanse the lepers, raise the dead, cast out devils: freely ye have received, freely give (Matthew 10:6-8).*

Yes He spoke this to the disciples, but you also have been commissioned to go forth and heal the sick, cleanse the lepers, raise the dead, cast out devils. To ignore this authority is to disobey the One who commissioned us. Jesus expects us to confront darkness, heal the sick, and set the oppressed free, not in our own power, but through His delegated authority.

The enemy is an opportunist. If you do not actively enforce your victory in Christ, the enemy will try to steal, kill, and destroy (John 10:10) everything god has given you even your life. The devil will take what you don't guard. Authority must be exercised to resist him. James 4:7 tells us, *"Submit yourselves, then, to God. Resist the devil, and he will flee from you."* The authority Jesus gave you is your weapon. Use it.

Walking in your Kingdom authority is a defense against identity theft. The enemy's strategy is to distort your view of who you are in Christ. But when you exercise your authority, you affirm your identity as a co-heir with Christ, seated in heavenly places (Ephesians 2:6). Every time you stand in your authority, you are declaring: *"I know who I am, and I know whose I am."*

Your authority is not just for you. It is for others. People in your family, workplace, and community need someone who can stand in faith, pray with boldness, and speak life with confidence. Romans 8:19 tells us, *"For the creation waits in eager expectation for the children of God to be revealed."* When you rise in spiritual authority, it creates space for others to be set free.

We don't carry authority just to defend ourselves, we use it to advance the Kingdom and take territory for Heaven. When you proclaim the Gospel, cast out demons, and declare the Word of God, you are pushing back darkness and advancing God's rule on the earth. Matthew 11:12 says, *"From the days of John the Baptist until now, the kingdom of heaven suffers violence, and the violent take it by force."* Exercising your authority means you're not waiting passively. You're taking ground.

Every act of spiritual authority is a reminder to the enemy that he is defeated. When you rebuke fear, command healing, or intercede with power, you reinforce what Jesus accomplished on the cross. Colossians 2:15 tells us, *"Having disarmed the powers and authorities, He made a public spectacle of them, triumphing over them by the cross."* You don't fight *for* victory. you fight *from* victory. And every time you use your authority, hell is reminded that Jesus has already won.

Your life is a message. People should look at your life and see a living preview of Heaven's reality. Your love should reflect Christ's love. Your peace should reflect Heaven's calm. Your boldness should reflect the confidence of your King. You are not here to blend in. You are here to represent a higher Kingdom. You were born to rule. God's original design for humanity was dominion (Genesis 1:26-28). Sin disrupted that rule, but Jesus restored it. Now, as citizens of the Kingdom, we've been re-commissioned to walk in dominion not over people, but over darkness, disorder, and deception.

You are not weak, voiceless, or invisible. You've been given authority for such a time as this. To stay silent is to surrender ground. To shrink back is to give the enemy permission. You've been given the keys; don't leave them hanging unused. The battle is real, but so is your authority. Rise up, speak out, and take your place as a Kingdom ambassador, clothed in power and backed by Heaven. Exercise your Kingdom authority in daily. You don't need to be in a pulpit to walk in authority. You just need to be in position.

When you pray in faith, expect Heaven to respond. When you declare God's Word over your home, family, or city, When you stand firm against fear, temptation, and demonic oppression, when you speak life in atmospheres of despair and hopelessness, When you refuse to bow to culture and instead reflect Kingdom truth You are exercising Kingdom authority.

Stop allowing your circumstances to dictate your peace. Stop tolerating what God didn't authorize. Stand your ground and bring Heaven's order into chaos. This isn't about controlling people. It is about enforcing Heaven's agenda.

Heaven is looking for those who will rise up, take their place, and release God's will into the earth. Will you be one?

Living in Kingdom authority means walking in the same authority that Jesus exercised while He was on earth. It's not about striving or forcing results, but about recognizing and partnering with the authority you've been given as a son or daughter of the King.

How To Exercise Kingdom Authority In Your Daily Life

Also, living in Kingdom authority is not just about understanding it intellectually. It is about actively applying it in your everyday circumstances. Here are some practical exercises and step-by-step examples to help you walk in the authority that God has given you.

1. Walking in Authority Over Your Thoughts

Your mind is one of the primary places where the battle for your authority is fought. The enemy wants to steal, kill, and destroy by planting lies, doubts, and fear in your thoughts. But the Kingdom mindset is one of peace, confidence, and power, rooted in the truth of who you are in Christ. When negative or destructive thoughts arise (such as fear, doubt, anxiety, or anger), use your Kingdom authority to take them captive and bring them into alignment with God's Word.

Step-by-Step Example:

- **Step 1: Recognize** the thought as contrary to God's truth. For example, if you feel anxious about a situation, recognize that the Kingdom of God is one of peace, not anxiety.

- **Step 2: Declare the truth.** Speak out loud: "I am a child of God, and I have the peace of Christ. I take authority over this anxiety in the name of Jesus."

- **Step 3: Replace the thought.** Instead of continuing to dwell on the fear, declare God's promises over the situation. For instance, *"God has not given me a spirit of fear, but of power, love, and a sound mind"* (2 Timothy 1:7).

- **Step 4: Visualize** your mind being renewed. Picture the anxiety being replaced with peace as you focus on God's truth.

Scripture:

- *"We demolish arguments and every pretension that sets itself up against the knowledge of God, and we take captive every thought to make it obedient to Christ." (2 Corinthians 10:5 NIV)*

2. Exercising Authority Over Your Emotions

Emotions are powerful, but they are not meant to control you. As a believer, you have the authority to choose your responses, no matter how you feel. When anger, anxiety, fear, and other emotions arise, you can bring them under the submission of Christ's peace.

Step-by-Step Example:

- **Step 1: Recognize** the thought as contrary to God's truth. For example, if you feel anxious about a situation, recognize that the Kingdom of God is one of peace, not anxiety.

- **Step 2: Declare the truth.** Speak out loud: *"I am a child of God, and I have the peace of Christ. I take authority over this anxiety in the name of Jesus."* *"The peace of God, which transcends all understanding, will guard my heart and mind in Christ Jesus"* (Philippians 4:7).

- **Step 3: Replace the thought.** Instead of continuing to dwell on the fear, declare God's promises over the situation. For instance, *"God has not given me a spirit of fear, but of power, love, and a sound mind"* (2 Timothy 1:7).

- **Step 4: Command peace.** Jesus calmed the storm with His words, saying, *"Peace, be still"* (Mark 4:39). You can too. Declare peace over your mind and heart.

- **Step 5: Visualize** your mind being renewed. Picture the anxiety being replaced with peace as you focus on God's truth.

Scripture:

- *"We demolish arguments and every pretension that sets itself up against the knowledge of God, and we take captive every thought to make it obedient to Christ." (2 Corinthians 10:5 NIV)*

3. Walking in Authority in Your Relationships

Kingdom authority doesn't mean dominating others. It means loving and serving with the authority that comes from Heaven. You have authority in your relationships to speak life, bring healing, and establish peace.

Step-by-Step Example:

- **Step 1: Speak life.** Jesus used His words to heal and bring life. You can too. Speak words of encouragement and truth into the lives of those around you.

- **Step 2: Forgive quickly.** *"If you forgive the sins of any, they are forgiven"* (John 20:23).

Forgiveness is an exercise of authority, releasing people from the grip of offense.

- **Step 3: Pray with authority.** When someone is struggling, you can pray with confidence knowing that your prayers carry weight in the spiritual realm.

4. **Exercising Authority Over Your Words**

   Your words have power. In the Kingdom of God, words carry authority because they align with God's will. Speak life, not death, into situations, people, and circumstances.

   Step-by-Step Example:

   - **Step 1: Identify an area of need or concern** in your life. This could be your finances, relationships, health, or work.

   - **Step 2: Speak a declaration of authority** over that area. Declare positive, Kingdom-centered declarations over yourself, your family, and your environment. For example, *"I declare that my finances are blessed and will multiply to advance God's Kingdom."*

   - **Step 3: Stand firm in your declaration.** Don't waver. Every time a negative thought or fear arises about that situation, speak the truth of

God's Word instead.

- **Step 4: Pray with authority.** Command situations to change in alignment with God's will. For example: *"I command every financial burden to be removed, in Jesus' name. I receive God's provision now."*

Scripture:

- *"I tell you the truth, if anyone says to this mountain, 'Go, throw yourself into the sea,' and does not doubt in their heart but believes that what they say will happen, it will be done for them."* (Mark 11:23 NIV)

5. **Exercising Authority Over Your Environment**

   Your environment is a reflection of your authority in Christ. Whether it's your home, workplace, or community, you can shape the atmosphere by walking in Kingdom authority. Declare the peace of God over your home, workspace, or any area that feels out of alignment.

   Step-by-Step Example:

   - **Step 1: Identify the environment** that needs change. Is it a tense work atmosphere? A chaotic home? An anxious family member?
   - **Step 2: Walk into the area** and speak peace

over it. For example, *"In the name of Jesus, I declare peace and unity in this home/workplace. I bind every spirit of division, fear, and chaos, and I loose peace, harmony, and God's will to reign here."*

- **Step 3: Invite the Holy Spirit** into the environment by praying, *"Holy Spirit, take charge. Let Your presence fill this room and bring God's Kingdom into every corner of this space."*

- **Step 4: Observe and affirm.** Watch as the atmosphere begins to shift. Continue to speak peace and declare God's truth over the space regularly.

Scripture:

- *"Peace be to this house." (Luke 10:5 NKJV)*

6. **Exercising Authority in Healing and Deliverance**

   As a believer, you have authority over sickness, disease, and demonic forces. You can pray and speak healing and deliverance into any situation. Use your Kingdom authority to pray for healing for yourself or others.

   Step-by-Step Example:

- **Step 1: Identify the need.** Is it someone in your family suffering from illness? Or do you need healing for yourself?

- **Step 2: Lay hands** on the person or on yourself if you're praying for your own healing.

- **Step 3: Declare the healing power of God.** For example: *"By His stripes, you are healed. I command every spirit of infirmity to leave in Jesus' name. I release the healing power of God over this body, and I declare restoration."*

- **Step 4: Believe in the authority of your words.** Stand firm in your belief that healing is happening, whether or not you immediately see the manifestation.

Scripture:

- *"And these signs will follow those who believe: In My name they will cast out demons; they will speak with new tongues; they will take up serpents; and if they drink anything deadly, it will by no means hurt them; they will lay hands on the sick, and they will recover." (Mark 16:17-18 NKJV)*

7. Exercising Authority in Stewardship

Kingdom authority also applies to how you manage God's resources. You have the authority to prosper, to manage finances, and to steward God's blessings for His Kingdom. Steward your finances, time, and talents with the understanding that they belong to God.

Step-by-Step Example:

- **Step 1: Assess your finances, time, and resources.** Are you being a good steward of what God has given you?

- **Step 2: Commit to using your resources for God's glory.** For example, *"Lord, I dedicate my finances to You. Help me to manage them wisely and use them to bless others and advance Your Kingdom."*

- **Step 3: Give generously.** Practice tithing and generosity, knowing that as you give, you are partnering with God's Kingdom to expand His work.

- **Step 4: Declare abundance.** As you sow generously, declare: *"I am blessed to be a blessing. My finances are prospering to fulfill God's purpose for my life."*

Scripture:

- *"Give, and it will be given to you. A good*

measure, pressed down, shaken together and running over, will be poured into your lap. For with the measure you use, it will be measured to you." (Luke 6:38 NIV)

8. Exercising Authority Over Your Life's Purpose and Assignment

Every believer has a Kingdom assignment, and part of your authority is to walk confidently in that calling. Declare God's will over your life and step into your Kingdom assignment with confidence and authority.

Step-by-Step Example:

- **Step 1: Clarify your assignment.** What is God calling you to do in this season? Is it a specific ministry, business, or area of influence?

- **Step 2: Declare your calling.** Say: *"I am called to bring Heaven to earth. I am equipped and empowered by God to fulfill my purpose."*

- **Step 3: Take action.** Step forward in faith, whether it's launching a ministry, starting a project, or serving in your community.

Scripture:

- *"I can do all things through Christ who*

strengthens me." *(Philippians 4:13 NKJV)*

Additional Scriptures for Practical Application of Kingdom Authority:

Matthew 10:1 (NIV) – *"Jesus called His twelve disciples to Him and gave them authority to drive out impure spirits and to heal every disease and sickness."* You have been given authority to heal and cast out demons, not in your own strength, but through the power of the Holy Spirit.

- **Luke 10:19 (NIV)** – *"I have given you authority to trample on snakes and scorpions and to overcome all the power of the enemy; nothing will harm you."* The authority of Jesus is greater than any weapon or attack of the enemy. You are protected, and the power to overcome is within you.

- **Matthew 16:19 (NIV)** – *"I will give you the keys of the Kingdom of heaven; whatever you bind on earth will be bound in heaven, and whatever you loose on earth will be loosed in heaven."* You have the authority to bind and loose, to declare Heaven's will on earth.

- **Romans 8:17 (NIV)** – *"Now if we are children, then we are heirs—heirs of God and co-*

heirs with Christ, if indeed we share in His sufferings in order that we may also share in His glory." As an heir of God, you have inherited the authority and dominion of the Kingdom.

- **Mark 11:23-24 (NIV)** – *"Truly I tell you, if anyone says to this mountain, 'Go, throw yourself into the sea,' and does not doubt in their heart but believes that what they say will happen, it will be done for them."* Exercising authority through faith-filled words can move mountains in your life. Speak boldly, in faith, and with authority.

- **John 14:12 (NIV)** – *"Very truly I tell you, whoever believes in me will do the works I have been doing, and they will do even greater things than these, because I am going to the Father."* Jesus didn't just perform miracles; He empowered us to do the same—and even greater works—through the authority He's given us.

To walk in Kingdom authority is to recognize that you are not powerless. Through Jesus, you have been given both power and authority to represent Heaven on Earth. Your words, actions, and choices align with God's will and the power of the Holy Spirit to enforce it. You are a reigning one, carrying the authority to transform the world around you.

Reflection Questions:
1. Are there areas where you've tried to walk in authority without cultivating intimacy with Jesus?
2. How can you deepen your connection with the Holy Spirit?
3. Are you operating from a place of true spiritual weight, or just using the right words?

The Name of Jesus, the Word, and the Blood

As ambassadors of Heaven, we are not sent into the world empty-handed. God has not only given us the assignment to carry out His will on the earth, but He has also equipped us with the necessary weapons to walk in victory and authority. These weapons are not carnal but *"mighty through God to the pulling down of strongholds"* (2 Corinthians 10:4). Among the most powerful tools He has entrusted to us are the name of Jesus, the Word of God, and the Blood of Jesus. These are not religious phrases or mere traditions; they are *real spiritual weapons*, backed by Heaven's power and authority.

The Name Of Jesus

The name of Jesus is the most powerful name in all of heaven and earth. There is no name greater, higher, or more powerful than the name of Jesus. Throughout Scripture and Church history, we see the name of Jesus healing the sick, casting out demons, raising the dead, calming storms, and reassuring the fearful. Why? Because when we speak His name, we are not merely uttering a word we are invoking the very presence of the Living God. He is made present within us and among us, in all His power and love. His name carries His power, His authority, and His love.

The name "Jesus" literally means "God saves." It shares its roots with the Hebrew name "Yeshua" (Joshua), who led the Israelites into the Promised Land. Likewise, Jesus leads us into the ultimate Promised Land, eternal life, through His death and resurrection. Acts 4:12 reminds us, *"There is no other name under heaven given to mankind by which we must be saved."* His name is salvation. His name is victory. His name is power.

There's an old song I love, though I don't know who wrote it, that captures this beautifully:

In the name of Jesus, in the name of Jesus,
we have the victory.
In the name of Jesus, in the name of Jesus,
Satan, you have to flee.
Tell me, who can stand before us when we
call on that great name?
Jesus, Jesus, precious Jesus. We have the
victory.

The Reigning Ones

These words are not just poetic. They describe reality. Demons truly flee at the name of Jesus when it's spoken with conviction and faith. Satan is a liar, an accuser, and a deceiver, and he fears the name of Jesus, especially when it comes from the mouth of someone who truly knows its power. Too often, we take His name for granted or speak it without faith. But Jesus responds to faith. The more we recognize our dependence on Him, the truth that without Him we can do nothing, the more His power is released through us.

Praise is a powerful weapon. Even when you don't feel like praising, praise anyway. Praise shifts atmospheres. Praise silences the enemy. Praise invites the Holy Spirit to move freely, activating His gifts and releasing His presence. When you are a person of praise, when your heart is pure, and your faith is anchored in Christ, God can use you as a vessel of healing, deliverance, and breakthrough. Because you understand the power of His name and you pray it with boldness and belief.

> *"Therefore God exalted Him to the highest place and gave Him the name that is above every name, that at the name of Jesus every knee should bow, in heaven and on earth and under the earth."—Philippians 2:9-10 (NIV)*

The name of Jesus is not just a closing statement for prayers. It is the most powerful name in existence, given by the Father, exalted above every other name, and recognized in three realms: Heaven, earth, and hell. When you speak the name of Jesus, you are invoking the full authority, victory, and dominion of Christ Himself.

In the early church, miracles, deliverances, and salvations all took place through the declaration of Jesus' name. Peter declared to the lame man at the temple gate, *"In the name of Jesus Christ of Nazareth, walk"* (Acts 3:6), and power was released. The name of Jesus is not magical; it's authoritative. It must be spoken from a place of faith and covenant relationship.

When you declare Jesus' name over sickness, demonic oppression, or situations that need Heaven's intervention, you are standing as a deputized ambassador, speaking on behalf of the King. And hell must respond.

The Word of God and Its Power

The Word of God and Its Power

The Word of God is not just ink on pages or ancient stories from long ago. The Word of God is living, active, and supernatural. Hebrews 4:12 says,

"For the word of God is alive and active. Sharper than any double-edged sword, it penetrates even to dividing soul and spirit, joints and marrow; it judges the thoughts and attitudes of the heart." This means that God's Word has the divine ability to cut through confusion, expose deception, and bring clarity, healing, and direction.

The Word is God's voice in written form, a mirror that shows us who He is and who we are in Him. It is our spiritual food, our sword in warfare, our source of truth, and the foundation of our faith. It is through the Word that we come to know God's character, His promises, His will, and His ways. Without it, we are spiritually malnourished, vulnerable to lies, and unable to rightly discern truth from error.

The Word of God has creative power. In the beginning, God created the heavens and the earth *by His Word*. He spoke, and it was. Genesis chapter 1 shows us that what He speaks, He brings into existence. That same creative power is at work when we align our faith with His Word. When you declare what God has said, you are not speaking empty words; you are partnering with Heaven to see His will manifest on earth.

The Word of God is a weapon. Ephesians 6:17

calls the Word *"the sword of the Spirit."* This means that when you speak the Word in faith, you are wielding a divine weapon that pierces the enemy's lies and breaks strongholds. Jesus Himself used the Word to defeat Satan in the wilderness: "It is written..." (Matthew 4). He didn't argue. He didn't reason. He quoted truth, and the devil had to flee.

The Word of God transforms us. Romans 12:2 tells us, *"Do not conform to the pattern of this world, but be transformed by the renewing of your mind."* How do we renew our minds? By the Word of God. As we read it, meditate on it, and obey it, our thinking is reprogrammed. Lies are uprooted. Strongholds are broken. Our identity is restored. The Word changes us from the inside out.

The Word of God establishes our authority. Your authority in Christ is only as strong as your understanding of the Word. If you don't know what God has said, you won't know what belongs to you. Satan thrives on ignorance. But when you know the Word, you won't fall for his schemes. You can declare with confidence, *"It is written,"* and stand your ground with spiritual authority.

Therefore, we need to let the Word dwell in us. It

is not meant to sit on a shelf or be reserved for Sundays. It is your daily bread, your source of strength, your spiritual weapon. Let it dwell in you richly (Colossians 3:16). Speak it. Pray it. Declare it. Obey it. When the Word lives in your heart and flows from your mouth, you will walk in power, peace, and victory.

Praying Scripture is a powerful act of spiritual warfare. It moves your prayers from personal emotion to divine authority. When you decree God's Word, you are enforcing His will and advancing His Kingdom on earth. Don't just read the Word. Declare it, believe it, and stand on it. The Word gives your prayers substance and your authority foundation.

The Power of the Blood

As believers, we are not merely reciters of religious creeds; we are carriers of a living power. We have tasted and experienced the supernatural force of the blood of Jesus Christ. This blood is not symbolic tradition or spiritual superstition; it is a divine weapon that protects, delivers, redeems, and testifies. It ushers in new beginnings and draws a clear boundary between God's covenant people and the works of darkness.

The blood of Jesus is not just a theological principle; it is a living, speaking power. Scripture says, *"The blood speaks better things than that of Abel"* *(Hebrews 12:24)*. It speaks of forgiveness, of redemption, of healing, of victory. The enemy knows this, and he fears it. Satan is a legalist, always looking for grounds to accuse, condemn, and remind you of your past. But every time the blood is applied, his accusations are overruled.

When you invoke the blood of Jesus, you are standing on divine legal grounds. It's like an attorney standing before the court, making a plea based on undeniable evidence of the Cross. Jesus' slain body and shed blood are the eternal proof that sin has been defeated, death has been overcome, and Satan's power has been broken. Through the blood, you have the legal right to claim freedom from every accusation, curse, and spiritual bondage.

The blood doesn't just cover your past, it silences the accuser in the present and secures your victory for the future. When you plead the blood, you're not operating in fear; you are functioning from a place of dominion. You are enforcing what Jesus has already accomplished. The blood is your spiritual boundary, an unbreakable line that the enemy cannot cross.

Just as the Israelites were protected by the blood on their doorposts during the first Passover (Exodus

The Reigning Ones

12), so we are shielded by the blood of the Lamb. The destroyer may roam, but he cannot touch what has been marked by the blood. Whether you're facing demonic attack, mental oppression, physical illness, or emotional torment, invoke the blood. The blood of Jesus disarms every curse. It breaks every bondage and secures divine protection. It releases supernatural deliverance. It declares your forgiveness, freedom, and victory. Declare it over your home, your children, your health, your finances, your purpose, and your future.

This is not spiritual hype, it is heavenly reality. The blood of Jesus is your defense, your testimony, and your weapon. Use it boldly. Too often, the Name, the Word, and the Blood are reduced to religious jargon. But in the spirit realm, they are recognized and respected. These weapons are not clichés or "church phrases." They are Heaven's weapons, and every believer has been given full access to them.

- When you say the name of Jesus in faith, demons tremble.
- When you declare the Word of God, angels move.
- When you plead the blood, the accuser is silenced.

You've been given of the supernatural weapons,

and each one is forged in the Spirit:

- **Prayer and fasting** – spiritual dynamite that breaks chains (Matthew 17:21)
- **Worship** – a weapon of divine reversal that silences the enemy (2 Chronicles 20:22)
- **Faith** – your shield against every fiery dart (Eph. 6:16)

These are not symbolic, they are practical tools that shift the atmosphere, silence the accuser, and enforce Heaven's rule on Earth. We are to use them to enforce Christ's victory.

Walking in authority requires action. It's not enough to *know* about these weapons. You must *use* them. Authority is not activated by information but by revelation and obedience. You are in a battle, and you have been equipped to win. Don't let these spiritual tools sit on the shelf of your knowledge. Use them boldly, consistently, and with unwavering faith.

Declaration

Declare these aloud in faith:

- I walk in Kingdom authority.

- I have been given the name of Jesus, the Word of God, and the blood of Jesus as weapons of victory.
- I declare that every enemy must bow to the name of Jesus.
- I speak the Word with faith and authority, and it does not return void.
- I plead the blood of Jesus over every area of my life and stand in victory.
- I am an equipped ambassador, and I walk in power, not fear. In Jesus' name, amen.

Prayer

Father, thank You for entrusting me with Kingdom authority. I repent for any way I've lived beneath what You've provided. Help me walk in boldness, obedience, and faith. Help me to recognize and resist the schemes of the enemy. Let Your power flow through me so that Jesus is glorified in every area of my life. In His name I pray, Amen.

Declaration

- I have been given authority in Christ.

- I am a Kingdom ambassador with Heaven's backing.
- I resist the enemy and stand firm in truth.
- I speak life, declare God's Word, and shift atmospheres.
- I walk in boldness, power, and dominion because I belong to the King.

The Holy Spirit and the Kingdom of God

"For the kingdom of God is not a matter of talk but of power." —1 Corinthians 4:20 (NIV)

The key to the Kingdom of God is the Holy Spirit. You cannot live with a Kingdom mindset apart from the Holy Spirit. He is not an optional extra to the Christian life but the very power source, voice, and administrator of God's reign on earth.

From Genesis to Revelation, the Spirit of God makes Heaven's will visible here below. He doesn't merely stir emotions, He establishes divine government. Wherever the Holy Spirit rules, the Kingdom of God is manifest. Wherever the Holy Spirit is ignored, true Kingdom power is absent.

Jesus never intended for you to try to live the Christian life without help. That's why He said, "It is to your advantage that I go away; for if I do not go away, the Helper will not come to you. But if I go, I will send Him to you" (John 16:7). That Helper is the Holy Spirit. Heaven's power living within you. He fills you with boldness (Acts 1:8), He guides you with wisdom (John 14:26), and convicts you in love (John 16:8). He teaches you to distinguish Kingdom truth from worldly counterfeits, so you can align every decision under the King's heart.

When Jesus walked the earth, He was full of the Spirit, led by the Spirit, and empowered by the Spirit (Luke 4:1-14). Every miracle, every declaration of the Kingdom, flowed through Him. Now that same Spirit dwells in you: Romans 8:11 says, *"The Spirit of God, who raised Jesus from the dead, lives in you..."* (NLT). On the day you believed and gave your life to Jesus, *"...having believed, you were sealed with the Holy Spirit of promise"* (Ephesians 1:13).

The Kingdom of God comes alive in your life when you yield to the Holy Spirit. Without Him, Kingdom life is just theory. With Him, it becomes experience. The Holy Spirit is not just about power. He's about intimacy. He reveals Jesus, and He glorifies the King (John 16:14). When you walk in step with the Spirit, you begin to think, act, and respond more like Jesus.

The Holy Spirit is your Kingdom compass. He brings conviction, not condemnation, so you stay aligned with the King's heart. He teaches and reminds you of God's Word, helping you walk in truth (John 14:26). He gives you discernment so you can tell the difference between what is of the Kingdom and what's of the counterfeit world.

The Kingdom comes through the Spirit. Jesus said, *"If I cast out demons by the Spirit of God, then the kingdom of God has come upon you"* (Matthew 12:28). Wherever the Holy Spirit is actively working, the Kingdom is being revealed. That means when healing breaks forth, when freedom comes to those bound, and when lives are transformed, the Kingdom is there. You don't need a title or a pulpit to operate in Kingdom power. You just need the Holy Spirit and obedience. His gifts, fruits, and leading are available to every believer who will yield.

The Holy Spirit doesn't come just to make you feel good. He comes to make you effective. He empowers you for purpose. Acts 1:8 says, *"But you will receive power when the Holy Spirit has come upon you; and you shall be My witnesses..."* So, Kingdom ambassadors aren't just informed; they are empowered to advance God's Kingdom.

The Holy Spirit fills you with:

- Boldness to speak God's truth.
- Wisdom to make godly decisions.
- Love to reflect Christ.
- Gifts to serve others supernaturally.
- Strength to overcome sin and trials.

Because the Spirit reigns in you, when you share your faith in Christ, the mustard seed of Kingdom truth you plant will grow beyond measure (Matthew 13:31-32). God's government is ever-expanding, its influence unstoppable, because it operates by Spirit rather than flesh. The Holy Spirit's indwelling presence, from the moment of conversion, is a believer's constant source of power and authority, enabling them to live a life of spiritual dominion.

Sensitivity to the Holy Spirit is the key to living Kingdom life. That means daily surrender, not just emotional moments during worship. The Spirit leads in the grocery store as much as in the prayer room. He will lead you in difficult conversations and give you what you should say if you ask Him. He will guide you in career decisions, parenting, and relationships. When the Spirit leads, peace follows. Even in the storm, you're anchored by the King's presence.

Colossians 3:15 says, *"Let the peace of Christ rule in your hearts."* The word "rule" implies the role of an umpire, someone who makes decisions and maintains order. This means peace should be the deciding factor in your decisions, guiding you like a referee who ensures everything stays in alignment. Instead of letting emotions, pressure, or personal desires lead you, God calls you to let His peace be the determining voice.

Here are a few practical ways to stay Spirit-led:

1. Begin your day with surrender. Ask the Holy Spirit to lead you.
2. Cultivate stillness. You won't hear His whisper when your life is loud.
3. Obey the voice of the Holy Spirit quickly. The more you respond to His prompting, the more clearly you'll hear Him.
4. Stay in the Word. The Spirit and the Word always agree.
5. You have been made holy. Walk in the holiness. Sin clouds your spiritual sensitivity. Keep your heart clean. Be quick to repent when you miss it.

Remember Jesus said, *"The kingdom of God is within you"* (Luke 17:21). That happens through the Holy Spirit. Heaven has already moved in. You are not powerless, and you are not alone. The Spirit of the living God dwells in you, and He's on a mission to reveal the rule and reign of Jesus through your life. When you say yes to the Holy Spirit, you're saying yes to Heaven's government operating in and through you. You become a living conduit of Kingdom reality.

Prayer

Holy Spirit, thank You for living in me. Fill every part of my life with Your presence. Help me how to walk in step with You. I surrender to Your leadership, Your power, and Your wisdom. Use me to release the Kingdom of God everywhere I go. I don't want to live by human strength. I want to live empowered, Spirit-filled, and Christ-centered. In Jesus' name, Amen.

Declaration

Declare these aloud in faith:

- The Spirit of God lives in me.
- I am empowered, not powerless.
- I am led by Heaven's wisdom.
- I operate in supernatural boldness and love.
- Through the Holy Spirit, the Kingdom of God is revealed in my life.

Living From God's Infinite Supply

"And my God will supply all your needs according to His riches in glory in Christ Jesus." —Philippians 4:19 (NASB)

One of the greatest shifts that happens when you embrace a Kingdom mindset is the way you view provision. In the world's system, supply is limited. In the Kingdom of God, provision is infinite because it flows from an inexhaustible Source, God Himself. So, in the Kingdom of God, lack is not your portion. Scarcity is not your inheritance. As a child of the King, you are called to live from the never-ending, abundant provision of your heavenly Father. This supply is not limited by economic conditions, inflation, or your paycheck. It flows from the very throne of God and is accessed by faith, stewardship, and alignment with Kingdom principles.

Although your country may experience economic downturns, inflation, job layoffs, and uncertainty,.

Heaven is not in recession. God is never in crisis. He is not wringing His hands trying to figure out how to bless you. He is not limited by your job title, your background, or your bank account. Psalm 50:10-12, signifies that God is the ultimate owner and provider, possessing all resources and not needing anything from people.

As a child of God and a citizen of Heaven, you have access to Heaven's supply through faith, obedience, and alignment with Kingdom principles. You are an heir walking in inheritance, not an orphan trying to survive. God's supply is limitless, not lacking in any resource. He owns the cattle on a thousand hills (Psalm 50:10). Psalm 24:1 says, *"The earth is the Lord's, and everything in it."*

The Kingdom mindset recognizes that we are not the owners of our time, talents, abilities, relationships, our treasure, and even our lives. Everything we possess, from wealth to influence, from revelation to spiritual gifts, and your purpose has been entrusted to us by God for a divine purpose, and we are accountable for how we manage them. (1 Corinthians 4:1-2, 1 Peter 4:10).

1st Chronicles 29:12 declares: *"Wealth and honor come from you; you are the ruler of all things. In your hands are strength and power to exalt and give strength to all."* This truth confronts one of the most subtle yet dangerous deceptions of our time, the idea that we are self-made or that our success comes solely from our effort. Yes, we labor, and we make choices, but even the strength to work, the wisdom to lead, and the opportunities we receive come from God. He is both the source and sustainer of all things.

God's supply always flows in alignment with His assignment. When you pursue your divine purpose, expect God to fund it. Jesus taught this principle in Matthew 6:33: *"Seek first the kingdom of God and His righteousness, and all these things will be provided for you."* 2 Peter 1:3 states that God has given believers everything needed for life and godliness through knowledge of Him.

"All these things" refers to every need you have, be it food, clothing, shelter, money, or whatever. God isn't saying your needs don't matter. He's saying your priorities matter. When your heart is fixed on Kingdom purposes, provision follows. This is not prosperity gospel; it is Kingdom alignment. God takes care of His own. He funds what He births. He supplies what He sends.

Supernatural provision is real. Throughout Scripture, we see God providing in miraculous ways:

- Manna in the wilderness (Exodus 16)
- Oil that didn't run out (2 Kings 4)
- Food multiplied to feed thousands (Mark 6)
- Taxes paid with a coin from a fish's mouth (Matthew 17:27)

The same God who did it then still does it now. He knows how to meet needs in ways you could never predict. When you walk by faith and obedience, you create space for supernatural supply.

One of the greatest revelations a believer can embrace is that God owns everything. In the Kingdom, stewardship isn't just about money; it's about everything Heaven places in your hands. Psalm 24:1 says, *"The earth is the Lord's, and everything in it."* The Kingdom mindset recognizes that we are not the owners of our time, talents, abilities, relationships, our treasure, and even our lives. Everything we possess, from wealth to influence, from revelation to spiritual gifts, and your purpose has been entrusted to us by God for a divine purpose, and we are accountable for how we manage them. (1 Corinthians 4:1-2, 1 Peter 4:10).

The Reigning Ones

When Jesus taught us to pray, He said, "Give us this day our daily bread," not because God needs reminding, but because He wants us to daily expect His provision. You were not designed to live under stress, lack, or barely getting by. That's the curse Jesus broke on the cross. You were designed to live in sync with Heaven, where there is no shortage. God wants you prosperous. The enemy wants you broke.

The devil's strategy is simple: keep you broke so you can't build the Kingdom. If he can convince believers that poverty is holy or that wealth is evil, he effectively cripples the Church from funding missions, feeding the poor, building churches, or helping the broken. The enemy doesn't care if you go to church or if you go to heaven, as long as you're ineffective on earth. He works overtime through bad theology, religious tradition, and manipulative teaching to make people believe that money is inherently wrong.

The "prosperity gospel" has been twisted on both ends. On one side, it's been abused for personal gain. On the other, it's been demonized to keep believers in fear of financial blessing. But the truth is, money is a tool, and when it's in the hands of righteous people, it builds hospitals, sends missionaries, funds orphanages, rescues women from trafficking, and spreads the Gospel across nations. Wealth is a weapon when used for Kingdom purposes.

True prosperity is not about acquiring material things for selfish pleasure. It's about living in the fullness of God's provision so that you can fulfill His purpose on the earth. 3 John 1:2 says, *"Beloved, I pray that you may prosper in all things and be in health, just as your soul prospers."* This shows us that soul prosperity, internal alignment with God's truth, is the foundation for outward abundance.

Prosperity begins by putting God first, committing to do life His way, and trusting that He will provide. It means believing He wants to bless you abundantly, not just so you can have more, but so you can do more for His glory.

Faith and Action Produce Results

Everything in the Kingdom works by faith. But faith is not passive. James said, *"Faith without works is dead"* (James 2:26). Faith speaks, sows, and steps. Faith expects God to show up but also moves in obedience. That's why Jesus said in Mark 11:24, *"Whatever you ask in prayer, believe that you have received it, and it will be yours."* You must believe it before you see it.

That belief transforms your mindset. Proverbs 23:7 says, *"As a man thinks in his heart, so is he."* If you constantly see yourself as broke, as barely making it, as not worthy of blessing, that mindset will manifest in your life. But when you renew your mind to the truth of Kingdom abundance, your external world begins to shift.

Living from God's infinite supply is not about greed. It's about grace. It's not about luxury. It's about legacy. As a citizen of the Kingdom, you have access to an endless flow of provision. You don't live from a paycheck, a budget, or an economy. You live from Heaven's supply, and it never runs dry.

Break the mindset that glorifies lack and embrace the truth that your Father owns it all. Prosperity isn't a side topic; it's a spiritual reality tied to purpose, obedience, and Kingdom vision. And when you align with that truth, you'll begin to walk in supernatural abundance, not just for yourself, but for everyone God has called you to impact. In God's Kingdom, we don't purchase provision, we believe for it. Faith activates Heaven's flow. Faith is the currency of the Kingdom.

Jesus continually responded to faith, not need.

Many people had needs, but it was faith that unlocked miracles. When you live from God's supply, you stop panicking when the numbers don't add up. You learn to trust that God sees, He knows, and He provides. Your job, or your business is a resource, but it is not your Source. God may use a job, business, investment, or even the generosity of others to meet your needs, but never confuse the channel with the Source.

Living with a Kingdom mindset means recognizing that everything you have is from God and for God. It means you don't cling to things; you steward them. You don't hoard; you give freely, trusting that your Father always has more. You give generously, even when it doesn't make sense. You obey, even when the instructions seem risky. You tithe and sow, not out of legalism, but out of faith in your Source.

Many believers are saved but still think like beggars, hoping for scraps instead of living from the overflow of Heaven. Though redeemed by Christ, they continue to operate with a mindset shaped by lack, fear, and survival. But as children of God, we are not orphans or beggars. We are heirs to the Kingdom, with access to divine provision, wisdom, and favor. The way we think determines how we live. Transformation begins when we shift from a poverty mentality to a Kingdom mindset rooted in truth.

This table contrasts the thoughts of a lack mindset with the truths of an abundance mindset, anchored in the unshakable promises of God's Word.

Lack Mindset	Abundance Mindset	Scripture Promise
"There's never enough for me."	"God is my source; He supplies all I need."	"And my God will supply all your needs according to His riches in glory..." (Phil. 4:19)
"I can't afford to be generous."	"God blesses me to be a blessing to others."	"You will be enriched in every way so that you can be generous on every occasion..." (2 Cor. 9:11)
"I have to fight for every opportunity."	"What God has for me is for me. I rest in His timing."	"No good thing will He withhold from those who walk uprightly." (Psalm 84:11)
"If they win, I lose."	"There is room for everyone in God's Kingdom."	"Rejoice with those who rejoice..." (Romans 12:15)
"I'm always behind."	"God's timing is perfect; I'm right where I need to be."	"He has made everything beautiful in its time." (Ecclesiastes 3:11)

"I'll never get out of this debt."	"With wisdom and discipline, God will lead me to financial freedom."	*"The borrower is servant to the lender,"* (Prov. 22:7) + *"You shall lend and not borrow."* (Deut. 28:12)
"People like me don't prosper."	"I am blessed because I belong to God's family."	*"You are Abraham's seed and heirs according to the promise."* (Galatians 3:29)
"I have to hold on to what I have—just in case."	"I trust God as my provider, so I can sow freely."	*"Give, and it will be given to you..."* (Luke 6:38)
"Nothing ever works out for me."	"All things are working together for my good."	*"All things work together for good..."* (Romans 8:28)
"I'll never have enough to fulfill my calling."	"God equips me with all I need for every good work."	*"God is able to bless you abundantly... in all things at all times..."* (2 Cor. 9:8)

You were not meant to live in survival mode. In Christ, you're called to live in abundance, not just for yourself, but to become a channel of blessing for others. As you reflect on the contrasts above, remember this: transformation doesn't happen overnight, but it begins with renewing your mind daily through the Word of God. Every time you choose to reject a lie and embrace the truth, you are stepping further into your identity as a Kingdom ambassador.

God says in 2 Corinthians 9:11 *"You will be enriched in every way so that you can be generous on every occasion..."* (NIV). God has not called you to barely get by. He has called you to live from His abundance, operate in His authority, and walk in peace, purpose, and power. Shift your thinking, and your life will follow. The Kingdom is within you, now it's time to live like it. Remember God's supply isn't about accumulation. It is about distribution. You're blessed to be a blessing.

God is not stingy. He is a lavish, generous Father who delights in meeting your needs and using you to meet the needs of others. His supply never runs dry. As you align with His Kingdom, provision will follow your purpose.

Practical Steps to Live From God's Supply

1. **Prioritize God's Kingdom**. Seek His heart and His will above material concerns.
2. **Steward well**. Budget wisely, avoid unnecessary debt, and manage what you have with integrity.
3. **Give generously**. Tithing, giving, and sowing are faith-acts that unlock spiritual flow.
4. **Speak life**. Refuse to speak words of lack. Declare what God says about His provision.

5. **Trust the process.** God's provision often comes in stages. Stay faithful in the waiting.

When you live from God's infinite supply, you bring glorify God and become a living testimony that Heaven is enough.

Stewardship

Living from God's supply doesn't mean we escape responsibility or stewarding well. It means we stop striving from a place of lack and start living from a place of overflow. Heaven's economy is not based on scarcity but on abundance. God doesn't bless hoarders. He blesses stewards. Stewardship means managing well what God has already given you, and generosity is the evidence that you trust the Source more than the supply. When you give, you're saying, "God, I believe there's more where that came from." We'll talk more about this later.

Luke 6:38 says, *"Give, and it will be given to you: good measure, pressed down, shaken together, and running over."* Increase comes when you open your hands, not when you close your fists. The Kingdom operates on seedtime and harvest, and your giving is the seed that unlocks supernatural harvest.

You don't need to be rich to be generous. You just

need a willing heart. The widow with two coins gave more than the rich because her giving was rooted in faith and sacrifice. And God saw it.

Money in itself is neutral, but in the hands of a righteous believer, it becomes a weapon for transformation. Your wealth is not for your comfort alone. It is for Kingdom advancement. It's to fund visions, support ministries, help the poor, and leave a legacy of faith.

Deuteronomy 8:18 reminds us, *"It is God who gives you the power to get wealth, that He may establish His covenant."* Wealth has a purpose: to establish God's Kingdom on the earth.

When you understand this, you stop chasing money and start pursuing purpose. And as you seek first the Kingdom and His righteousness, all these things, resources, opportunities, and connections will be added to you (Matthew 6:33).

The Parable of the Talents lets us know that God expects return on what he entrusts to us. Jesus gives us a clear picture of stewardship in Matthew 25:14-30. In the Parable of the Talents, a master entrusts his servants with wealth while he is away. Upon his return, he rewards those who multiplied what they were given. But the one who buried his talent out of fear is rebuked, not because he lost what was given, but because he failed to invest it.

> *"You wicked, lazy servant! [...] You should have put my money on deposit with the bankers, so that when I returned I would have received it back with interest."* (Matthew 25:26-27)

While the Parable of the Talents focuses on money, its core message is that God expects a return on all that He entrusts to us. God desires multiplication, not stagnation. Good stewardship is not simply about preservation. It is about advancement of His Kingdom.

Jesus challenges us with a choice in Matthew 6:19-21. He said *"Do not store up for yourselves treasures on earth... But store up for yourselves treasures in heaven..."* Where your treasure is, there your heart is. The way we use our resources reveals the true location of our hearts. If we are building our own empires, chasing worldly success, or hoarding wealth, we are serving mammon, not God. But when we invest in eternal things such as missions, justice, the local church, the poor, the Gospel we are declaring our allegiance to the Kingdom of God. *"No one can serve two masters... You cannot serve both God and money."*

Jesus said in Matthew 6:24. The early church modeled Kingdom stewardship. In Acts 4:32-35, we read of believers who sold property and possessions so that no one among them had need. They understood that what they had was not their own. it belonged to God. Their generosity was not driven by law, but by love and conviction. *"There was not a needy person among them..."* (Acts 4:34).

This is a powerful testimony to what can happen when the people of God embrace Kingdom-minded stewardship: communities are transformed, needs are met, and the love of Christ is revealed through radical generosity.

Everyone is a steward, whether they acknowledge God or not. Every human being is a steward because everything belongs to God. What differentiates faithful stewards from unfaithful ones is recognition of the Owner and alignment with His will.

Time is one of the greatest Kingdom resources we have. Unlike money, we can't earn more of it. Once spent, it's gone. As Christians and Kingdom ambassadors our influence, leadership, and relationships must reflect God's heart and priorities. When you adopt a Kingdom mindset, you stop asking, "What do I want to do with my life?" and you start asking,

"Lord, what would You have me do with what You've given me?" That shift in thinking is where true Kingdom stewardship begins.

Stewarding your time means aligning your calendar with Heaven's priorities. It means being intentional with how you spend your days, who you give your energy to, and what gets your attention. God entrusts you with purpose. Your calling is a trust. Your spiritual gifts are a trust. Your influence, no matter how big or small, is a trust. The Kingdom mindset doesn't let distractions determine direction. It redeems the time because the days are evil (Ephesians 5:16).

God also entrusts you to steward your finances with a kingdom mindset. Money is one of the clearest tests of stewardship. Jesus said, *"Where your treasure is, there your heart will be also"* (Matt. 6:21). In other words, your bank statement often reveals your true priorities.

God is not against wealth. He is against waste, greed, and idolatry. He wants you to prosper, but not at the expense of your soul. Stewardship means using money to serve God, not serving money as your god.

The Kingdom steward gives generously, saves

wisely, spends purposefully, and lives with open hands. God blesses good stewards so they can be channels, not reservoirs. If He can get it through you, He will get it to you. The world doesn't need more people waiting to be discovered. It needs more people stewarding their calling in faith, even when no one's watching.

God Rewards and honors faithful stewardship. In Luke 16:10, Jesus said, *"Whoever is faithful with little will also be faithful with much."* Your faithfulness now is preparing you for promotion later.

God doesn't waste obedience. He multiplies it. Even when it feels like no one sees what you're doing, Heaven sees. Every act of faithfulness, every private yes, every seed sown in secret is noted by the King. He is a rewarder not of talent, but of trust.

Keep in mind that you were created on purpose for a purpose. Your talents, passions, and spiritual gifts are not random, they are divine deposits meant to bring Heaven's influence to Earth. Romans 12:6 reminds us that *"we have different gifts, according to the grace given to each of us."*

The question is: Are you developing and using what God has given you?

- Have you laid your gifts at His feet?

- Are you faithful with the little things?
- Are you growing in your calling, or burying it?

At the end of this life, you won't be evaluated by how much you accumulated, but how faithfully you stewarded what was given. The Kingdom mindset lives for the *"Well done, good and faithful servant."* Not the applause of man, the validation of platforms, the accumulation of stuff, but the pleasure of the King.

Questions for Reflection

1. What lies or limiting beliefs about money and prosperity have you believed that may be keeping you from experiencing God's full provision?

2. How has fear, religion, or past teaching shaped your view of wealth and the role it plays in the Kingdom of God?

3. Are there areas of your life where you've been operating from a scarcity mindset rather than trusting in God's infinite supply?

4. In what ways can you grow in stewardship and generosity right now, even with what you currently have?

5. How can you begin to use your wealth, or the

resources God has given you as a tool for greater Kingdom impact?

Prayer

Father, I thank You that You are Jehovah Jireh, my Provider. You own it all, and nothing is too hard for You. Today, I repent for every mindset, belief, or fear that has kept me from trusting in Your abundant provision. I reject the lies of poverty, lack, and limitation. I choose to believe that prosperity is my birthright as Your child and that You delight in blessing me so that I can be a blessing.

Teach me to steward well what You've given me. Make me faithful with little so You can trust me with much. Use me as a vessel of generosity, integrity, and wisdom. Help me to walk by faith, to sow with expectation, and to speak life over my finances. I declare that I live from Your infinite, supernatural, unstoppable, and overflowing supply. I give You all the glory. In Jesus' name, Amen.

Declaration

Declare these aloud in faith:

- I live from Heaven's supply, not from the

world's systems.

- God is my Source, and I trust Him to meet all my needs abundantly.

- I break agreement with the poverty mindset and embrace Kingdom prosperity.

- I am a faithful steward and a joyful giver. Increase flows through my life.

- Wealth is a tool in my hands to build the Kingdom and bless others.

- I prosper in all things, even as my soul prospers.

- Lack is not my portion. I walk in supernatural provision and divine favor.

- Through faith and obedience, I see God's promises manifest in my finances.

The Power of Kingdom Fellowship

"And let us consider how we may spur one another on toward love and good deeds, not giving up meeting together, as some are in the habit of doing, but encouraging one another—and all the more as you see the Day approaching." —Hebrews 10:24-25 (NIV)

The Kingdom is about relationship. At the heart of the Kingdom of God is relationship. God, in His essence, is a relational being: Father, Son, and Holy Spirit. The perfect fellowship within the Trinity sets the model for the fellowship believers are meant to have with each other. The community of believers is called to reflect the relationship God has with Himself a relationship marked by love, unity, and mutual support.

In the Kingdom of God, relationships are a divine calling. We are meant to live and grow in fellowship with one another, because, as believers, we are not just individuals with separate lives. We are members of one body, connected to each other through Christ.

Kingdom fellowship is about more than just attending church services together; it's about sharing life, supporting one another, and encouraging each other in our walk with God.

Jesus prayed for His disciples, and by extension, for us, in John 17:21: *"That all of them may be one, Father, just as you are in me and I am in you."* The unity and love shared between the Father and Son is the same unity and love that God desires for His people. So, fellowship is an essential part of the Christian walk. It is not meant to be a solitary journey, but a collective mission. We need each other to walk it out.

Through relationships with fellow believers that we find encouragement, accountability, and support. In the early church, we see the beauty of this kind of fellowship. Acts 2:42-47 describes how the early believers "devoted themselves to the apostles' teaching and to fellowship, to the breaking of bread and to prayer." They were united in purpose and love, sharing everything in common, and this fellowship empowered them to spread the Gospel and live out the Kingdom.

In the same way, we are called to surround ourselves with believers who can help us grow in our faith, hold us accountable, and encourage us when life becomes difficult. Fellowship within the body of

Christ strengthens us and reminds us that we are not alone in this journey.

Fellowship is not only for personal growth; it is also vital for the advancement of God's Kingdom. When believers come together in unity and love, we create a powerful witness to the world around us. Jesus said in John 13:35, *"By this everyone will know that you are my disciples, if you love one another."* The love we share in fellowship is a testimony to the world that the Kingdom of God is real and alive.

When we build strong relationships with other believers, we begin to live out the culture of Heaven. The early church demonstrated this Kingdom culture as they lived in harmony, cared for one another, and shared their resources. Their fellowship was an attraction to others, drawing them into the Kingdom. When we live in community, we reflect the love and power of God to a watching world.

Practical Ways to Cultivate Kingdom Fellowship

Building strong, Kingdom-centered relationships requires intentionality and effort. Fellowship doesn't just happen; it's something we actively participate in, whether within the church or in our daily lives. Here are a few practical ways to cultivate Kingdom fellowship:

- **Prioritize Regular Gathering.** The early church gathered frequently to share life, pray, and support one another. Hebrews 10:25 encourages us not to forsake "meeting together." Whether it's attending church, joining a small group, or simply spending time in prayer with other believers, regular fellowship is key to staying connected.

- **Be Vulnerable and Authentic.** True fellowship requires vulnerability. It's easy to present a polished version of ourselves, but real, life-changing fellowship happens when we are honest about our struggles, fears, and weaknesses. When we open up, we allow others to pray for us, encourage us, and help us grow.

- **Serve One Another.** Fellowship is not just about receiving. It is also about giving. Kingdom fellowship is built on mutual care and service. Take time to serve others, whether it's through acts of kindness, prayer, or support during difficult times. The early church's fellowship was marked by a spirit of generosity, and we are called to do the same.

- **Encourage and Challenge One Another.** One of the most important aspects of fellowship is encouragement. We are called to "spur one another on toward love and good deeds" (Hebrews 10:24). This means not only offering words of encouragement but also challenging one another to grow, to live out our Kingdom purpose, and to remain faithful in the face of challenges.

- **Forgive and Reconcile.** In any community, misunderstandings and disagreements can arise. But Kingdom fellowship is built on a foundation of forgiveness and reconciliation. When conflict occurs, seek peace, extend grace, and work towards restoration. As Jesus said in Matthew 18:20, *"For where two or three are gathered in my name, there am I with them."* The presence of God is made known in our relationships, especially when we choose to forgive and reconcile.

When we embrace the power of Kingdom fellowship, we begin to experience the full richness of life in Christ. We become the hands and feet of Jesus, supporting one another and advancing the work of the Kingdom. Kingdom fellowship is about more than just being together, it's about building each other up in the faith and fulfilling our God-given purpose.

As we walk in fellowship, we are living examples

of what it means to be part of the family of God. We display the love, unity, and grace that reflect the heart of the Father. Through our relationships, we make the Kingdom of God tangible to those around us. As we fellowship with other believers, we show the world what it looks like to live in the unity and love of Christ.

Prayer

Father, thank You for the gift of fellowship. I am grateful for the relationships You have placed in my life. Help me to cultivate deeper connections with fellow believers and to be intentional in building Kingdom relationships. Help me to love, encourage, and serve others as You have loved and served me. May our fellowship be a reflection of Your love and an example of Your Kingdom to the world. In Jesus' name, Amen.

Declaration

Declare these aloud in faith:

- I am a member of the body of Christ.
- I will prioritize fellowship with other believers and commit to growing in unity and love.

- I will serve and encourage others, being a reflection of God's Kingdom on Earth.

- I will walk in forgiveness and reconciliation, fostering peace and harmony in my relationships.

- Through Kingdom fellowship, I will be strengthened and empowered to fulfill my God-given purpose.

Living with Dominion and Eternity in Mind

You were never created to live defeated, distracted, or directionless. As a child of God and a citizen of His Kingdom, you have been crowned with purpose, to reign in life through Christ and to live with eternity in view. These two truths go hand in hand. You walk in daily dominion not to build your own kingdom, but to reflect His. You live victoriously now because you live for what will last forever.

God does not want you to think and live like a victim. You have been brought out of darkness. It's time to step into your royal identity. God want you to reign on Earth. Jesus has restored your dominion, so you can live as a victorious ambassador of His Kingdom right now.

Romans 5:17 says, *"Those who receive the abundance of grace and the gift of righteousness will reign in life through the one man, Jesus Christ."* You walk in authority over the enemy.

The Reigning Ones

- You live above fear, sin, shame, and condemnation.

- You operate in freedom, confidence, and purpose.

- You reflect the character and culture of your King in everyday life.

You are not arrogant. You are in alignment with Christ. It's living under the rule of the King so you can release His rule on earth. It's praying with boldness, forgiving quickly, resisting temptation, and carrying peace into chaos. Your dominion is revealed in how you parent, how you speak, how you steward resources, and how you respond when no one's watching.

You have been moved from victim to victor. Your new identity in Christ has shifted everything. Your authority flows from your intimacy with the King. Now live sent. Live for what will last. Fix your eyes on eternity. 2 Corinthians 4:18 reminds us, *"We fix our eyes not on what is seen, but on what is unseen. For what is seen is temporary, but what is unseen is eternal."* You were not just made for dominion. You were made for destiny. And destiny is eternal.

This life is a vapor. This world is passing away, but

the Kingdom of God is unshakeable (Hebrews 12:28). We are ambassadors of the Kingdom of God sent to represent eternity in a world obsessed with the temporary. Let eternity become your lens. An eternal perspective frees you from the grip of distraction and comparison. It anchors you to what truly matters, which is pleasing God, loving others, and fulfilling your assignment.

Everything you do in Christ carries eternal weight. Even a small act of obedience will not be forgotten (Matt. 10:42).

Your Mission Is Where You Are

Many believers think "calling" means going to another nation or having a platform. But the Kingdom mindset says your mission is wherever your feet are. Your sphere of influence is your mission field. Wherever you are, Heaven has a strategy for that space, and you're part of it. Are you a teacher? You're on a mission. A stay-at-home parent? You're shaping the next generation of Kingdom carriers. A business owner? You're funding and influencing for the glory of God.

Don't be overwhelmed by the idea of being sent to distant lands or foreign countries. Don't underestimate the power of small, faithful steps. Revival doesn't always begin in stadiums. It often starts around kitchen tables, in coffee shops, and during conversations where love and truth collide.

While global missions are vital, the truth is that you have a mission field right where you are, in your home, at your workplace, in your neighborhood, and among your friends. Wherever you go, the Kingdom of God goes with you. The key is to recognize that your sphere of influence is your mission field.

On your job you represent the King through integrity, work ethic, and service. You show the world that work is not just for survival. It's a form of worship. In your family you represent the Kingdom through love, patience, and wisdom. You bring God's order and peace into your home. In your community you represent the Kingdom through acts of kindness, justice, and mercy.

You are the hands and feet of Jesus to those in need. In your church you represent the Kingdom through service, fellowship, and unity. You contribute to building a strong, Kingdom-minded community. Living sent means recognizing that every place you are is an opportunity to bring Heaven's influence to Earth.

Don't Wait. The Time Is Now

The world is growing darker, but your light is growing brighter. Now is not the time to shrink back. It's time to rise, represent Heaven, and fulfill the mission God has entrusted to you. Your life is a message. Your obedience is a weapon. Your faithfulness matters more than you think. Keep going. Keep growing. Keep seeking the Kingdom first (Matthew 6:33). Your impact won't always be visible on earth, but it will be eternal in Heaven. And one day, when this life fades and you stand before your King, may your heart be full of joy as He says: *"Well done, good and faithful servant. Enter into the joy of your Lord"* (Matthew 25:23).

On that day, titles won't matter. Faithfulness will. We will be rewarded not for how famous we were, but for how obedient we were. This truth shouldn't induce fear. It should ignite purpose. It should call you to live each day with the end in mind. Not just to reign, but to reign well. Not just to run, but to finish strong.

You've been crowned to reign and called to live with eternity in your heart. This is your moment. Not to chase success, but to carry significance. Not to shrink in fear, but to rise in faith. As Heaven's ambassador, your mission is to represent Jesus boldly, consistently, and faithfully. So, walk in your identity.

Reign in your sphere. And fix your eyes on the eternal. The Kingdom is within you. Now let it shine through you.

"The kingdom of God is not a matter of talk but of power." —1 Corinthians 4:20

Living with eternity in view doesn't make you impractical. It makes you unshakable. It orders your steps. It sharpens your focus. It helps you live not for "well known," but for "well done." It helps you live for the King's reward. Every believer will stand before Jesus, not to be condemned, but to give account (2 Corinthians 5:10).

Jesus said in Matthew 11:12, *"The Kingdom of Heaven suffers violence, and the violent take it by force."* You've been equipped to push back darkness, rescue the lost, and bring Heaven's reality to the earth. Don't wait for permission. God already gave it. Don't wait for perfection. God uses willing hearts. Don't wait for a better time. Now is the time. The Kingdom is advancing. Will you move with it?

Prayer

Father, thank You that I am not called to live beneath, but to reign in life through Jesus Christ.

Thank You for entrusting me with the mission of advancing Your Kingdom. I receive Your grace and righteousness. I surrender my life as a vessel of Your glory. Open my eyes to see the opportunities around me, and give me the boldness to represent You well. Let my words, actions, and presence bring light to dark places. Help me walk daily in authority and intimacy, to fix my eyes on what is eternal. Empower me to live for Your Kingdom, not just in word, but in power. May my life reflect Heaven and echo in eternity. In Jesus' name, Amen.

About The Author

Prophetess Angeline L. Williams is a submitted vessel of God who flows in the ministry gifts of prophet, evangelist, pastor, and teacher. God has led her to influence many individuals into a restored relationship with Jesus Christ. Her passion for God and His Word has led to an anointing to preach and teach the Word of God with authority, revelation, and deliverance. In 2002, she received her license and ordination to preach the gospel, assuming the roles of prophet, evangelist, pastor, and teacher.

She is the founder of Cyrus Redemption Center and Redeemed4Life Ministries. and a best-selling author whose books and sermons are illuminated with revelation, wisdom, and the healing power of testimony. Her books and messages are illuminated with revelation, personal testimony, and a depth of wisdom, and insight resulting from decades of study, and relationship with God.

She is also the owner of Williams DocuPrep, where she has been providing self-publishing services to authors, and independent publishers since 2005. If you are aspiring author and would like more info about how she can help you visit her website at www.williamsdocuprep.com to learn more.

"The Spirit of the Lord is upon me, because he hath anointed me to preach the gospel to the poor; he hath sent me to heal the brokenhearted, to preach deliverance to the captives, and recovering of sight to the blind, to set at liberty them that are bruised, to preach the acceptable year of the Lord." — Luke 4:18-19

See my other books here:
https://www.angelinelwilliams.com/my-books.html

Keep in touch with me here:
https://www.facebook.com/angeline.williams
https://www.instagram.com/msangelinew
https://www.youtube.com/@CRCFellowship